GCSE
CDT-DESIGN AND REALISATION

David Rees

Longman

GUIDES

COURSEWORK

LONGMAN COURSEWORK GUIDES

SERIES EDITORS
Geoff Black and Stuart Wall

TITLES AVAILABLE
Art and Design
Biology
Business Studies
CDT: Design and Realisation
Chemistry
Computer Studies
Economics
English
English Literature
Geography
Mathematics
Physics
Religious Studies
Science
Social and Economic History
World History

Longman Group UK Limited,
Longman House, Burnt Mill, Harlow,
Essex CM20 2JE, England
and Associated Companies throughout the world.

© Longman Group UK Limited 1989

First published 1989

British Library Cataloguing in Publication Data

Rees, David, 1932
    CDT.
    1. England. Secondary schools. Curriculum subjects:
    Crafts, design & technology. G.C.S.E. examinations.
    Techniques
    I. Title
    607'.6

    ISBN 0-582-05184-3

Produced by The Pen and Ink Book Company,
Huntingdon, Cambridgeshire

Set in 10/11pt Century Old Style

Printed and bound in Great Britain by
William Clowes Limited, Beccles and London

EDITORS' PREFACE

The introduction of GCSE created many challenges for both teachers and pupils, not least the idea that, for most subjects, the grade awarded should be based not only on examination performance but also on the assessment of certain pieces of coursework. Whilst this concept has been welcomed in most educational circles as relieving some or all of the stress associated with examinations, it is also recognised as imposing other sorts of pressures on pupils. To achieve good results, it is necessary to keep up to date, be organised, and most importantly, maintain an appropriate standard *from the beginning of the course*.

Longman Coursework Guides have been written by experienced examiners to give GCSE candidates help with such tasks as choosing, researching and writing up topics. In addition, the authors give many examples of (and comments upon) typical student assignments.

We believe that the books will stimulate as well as instruct, and will enable students to produce coursework which will truly reflect the level of commitment and effort which the GCSE demands.

Geoff Black and Stuart Wall

ACKNOWLEDGEMENTS

Grateful acknowledgement is made for the valuable support given by the following schools and their pupils whose work is used throughout the book:

Chestnut Grove School, London;
Haberdashers' School for Girls, Monmouth;
Rydal School Colwyn Bay;
Holyrood School, Chard;
Croesyceiliog Comprehensive, Croesyceiliog;
Filton High School, Bristol.

Appreciative acknowledgement is also due for permission to use examples of candidates' design work to the London and East Anglian Examination Group, and to the following for permission to quote extracts from their CDT syllabuses: London and East Anglian Examination Group; Midland Examining Group; Southern Examining Group; Northern Examining Association; Welsh Joint Education Committee.

My grateful thanks to Mike Rose for his constant support and inspiration as a Chief Examiner and friend.

My grateful thanks to Professor Syd Urry for his constant support and guidance.

Finally, my most grateful thanks to my wife Vivien, without whose devoted support my involvement in examining and writing would not be possible.

CONTENTS

THE ROLE OF COURSEWORK IN CDT

In subjects that have a practical element, i.e. where something has to be designed and made, the practical work is assessed and forms an important part of your final grade. Any subject with the prefix CDT involves the designing and making of a product and/or system. This practical element alone can contribute as much as 50% of the available marks. So you can see that what you do in lessons and at home is going to have an important effect upon your final assessment.

UNIT 1 THE IMPORTANCE OF COURSEWORK

If you look at Fig 1.1 you will see how much importance each Examining Group places upon coursework.

Group	Coursework	Written Exam	Design Paper	Design and Realisation
London and East Anglian Group (LEAG)	40%	30%	–	30%
Midland Examining Group (MEG)	30%	30%	–	40%
Northern Examining Association (NEA)	50%	20%	30%	–
Northern Ireland Schools Examinations Council (NISEC)	50%	20%	30%	–
Southern Examining Group (SEG)	50%	25%	25%	–
Welsh Joint Education Committee (WJEC)	50%	30%	20%	–

Fig 1.1
Importance of coursework in the assessment

★ For IGSE, see page 14

If you look at the first column, headed coursework, you can see what percentage of available marks is allocated to coursework. Four of the six Examining Groups allocate 50%; the other two allocate 40% and 30%. These two also have a Design and Realisation paper, which the others do not have, and which in many ways is very similar to coursework. It is similar to coursework in that something has to be designed and made, and the assignment is done in ordinary lesson time and any time you wish to spend on it at home. It is different in that the Examining Group sets the problem or problems to be resolved and you complete the assignment on paper supplied by the Group. So if you add the percentage in the final column to that in the first column you will see that for LEAG and for MEG the total from coursework-type activities is 70%. It would appear then that instead of these two groups offering a smaller percentage for coursework they are, in fact, offering more. But in order to understand how this works in practice, more detail is given later in this chapter.

1.1 The advantages of coursework

It has been recognised for a very long time that the hard work that is done in lesson time and at home often gets no direct reward, particularly in a system where everything depends on how well you perform in examinations. At the other extreme are subjects with no examinations set by the Examining Group. Here everything depends upon coursework. However, although subjects with the prefix CDT *do* place considerable importance upon coursework, a written examination still forms part of the method used to assess your ability.

Many people find it difficult to sit silently in a room and have problems in answering a lot of questions within a given space of time. Therefore the marks they receive may not necessarily be a true reflection of their ability. Under the pressure of an examination, silly mistakes can also be made, such as answering too many questions in one section and not enough in another. For the extra question that was answered no marks can be awarded, which is a heavy penalty for such a mistake. Also on the day of the examination you may be feeling very unwell so that no matter how hard you try to answer the questions you cannot perform at your best. However, in coursework you do have a chance of talking with others, not everything depends on how well you feel on the day and you do not have to work under the same pressure as in an examination. In addition, if you make a mistake there is often time to make a correction. So what you produce in coursework may be a fairer reflection of your true ability. Coursework can reveal personal qualities such as the *determination* and *perseverance* to see a task completed, and the degree of *initiative* used to overcome difficulties. Of course in many real-life situations we do have to work to tight time schedules, so work under timed examination conditions can certainly claim to also have merit in the overall assessment.

> **UNIT 2**

SKILLS TO BE TESTED THROUGH COURSEWORK

Design and Technology is really all about *solving problems* by a *practical means*. It is your ability to solve a problem, and to produce a product that solves that problem, that is assessed.

To arrive at a solution to a problem requires a number of quite different but related skills. For example, you need to have **design skills** that start with:

66 **Useful design skills.** 99

▶ an ability to *identify a need*
▶ an ability to *write a Design Brief*
▶ an ability to *write an analysis of the problem*.

These skills do not come easily and can be very daunting if you find yourself struggling to find a 'need'. What is a 'need'? *Needs* involve our basic requirements such as staying alive, being warm, having food to eat, buildings to protect us from the wet and cold weather, things that amuse us, and so on. Products are usually demanded because of the contribution they make to fulfilling a need. Even if a need has already been answered, then you may be able to find a modified or improved solution, so making it more efficient. Everything you see around you that is man-made is a solution to a need of some kind. If you consider a chair, it is a solution to a *need* to rest or support your body, rest your tired legs after a long walk, etc. Clearly some chairs are more comfortable than others and you may therefore be able to either modify an existing design or to come up with an alternative solution that is an improvement on the existing design.

66 **Try to identify a need at the beginning of the design process.** 99

Needs are all around you and where better to start than in the places with which you are familiar. For example in your home, at your school, or where you go with your friends for leisure, etc. The diagram below, which is an indication of the main areas, should help you find where a need may exist.

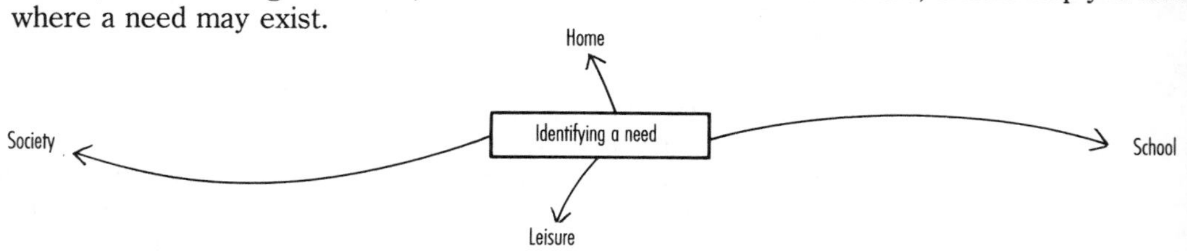

Home

Society ← Identifying a need → School

Leisure

Fig 1.2
The main areas where a need may exist

Take any one of these areas and put it in the centre of a page. Then add sub-groups to help you expand into areas that might yield a particular need, and best of all one that you will find interesting to resolve. For example, take *leisure* as a starting point. You might find that you will produce a page that contains the sub-areas shown in Fig 1.3.

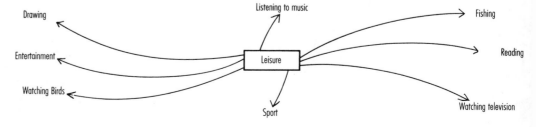

Drawing   Listening to music   Fishing

Entertainment   Leisure   Reading

Watching Birds   Watching television

Sport

Fig 1.3
Breaking an area down to find a particular need

If you now select a *particular* leisure activity that suits you, you can then take this a stage further. For instance, you could now put *sport* in the middle of a page and add the sub-areas of sport. This may seem a long way round, but it is a method you might try when you are having difficulty in identifying a need. It is also a method that can be *presented* with your work. It will show an assessor or examiner that you have looked at a wide range of possibilities and have carefully narrowed down your options *before* making a final decision.

Although you may have identified an area in which you are interested, you still have to identify a *problem*. The task now is to do some observing, perhaps to make notes and sketches, or even to take photographs of what you see. You will then have a record of the information you have collected. Again this can be presented as part of your coursework to show exactly *how* you set about finding a problem. Leonardo da Vinci (one of the world's greatest inventors who lived just over 460 years ago) said to his students who were looking for ideas, 'Open your eyes, it is all there for you to see.'

So far you will have been *demonstrating* your ability to identify a problem methodically, and to observe and record information. In recording you will be able to demonstrate your ability to sketch from first-hand experience, which is always harder than copying from a sketch that has been produced by someone else. Do not be tempted to spend a long time over these sketches and to colour them in to make them appear more presentable. This will be a waste of your time, taking time that could be more wisely spent on the next task, which is to write a Design Brief.

2.1   Writing a Design Brief

Many teachers find this a difficult task, so do not be surprised if you need to spend a little time in *selecting* what you need to say.

The word 'brief' can have two meanings: it can mean short, i.e. using not many words; and it can also mean information. When someone is being 'briefed' they are being given information. So if you join the two meanings you have a *short piece of information*. A good Design Brief should be concise and to the point, so when you write one you are demonstrating an ability to communicate concisely and clearly through the written word.

> **A good Design Brief is short and to the point.**

It is important to guard against writing statements that include the answer to the problem; e.g. 'Design a wooden table', 'Design an acrylic box', 'Design a milk bottle holder made from aluminium', etc. In the example of the wooden table, the need identified could have been expressed in more *general* terms, such as the need for a piece of furniture on which to place ornaments, a vase of flowers, etc. in the middle of a room. A small *wooden table* may be a good solution but having *stated* both the type of furniture and material for construction in the Design Brief, other possibilities have already been excluded. It would be better to write, 'Design a unit on which to stand ornaments and a vase of flowers'. There is then no mention of a preconceived idea of a table or that it should be made from wood. Use *broad terms* such as unit, fitting, container, support system, etc. rather than *specific terms* such as table, cupboard, box, television stand, etc.

> **In your Design Brief use broad terms which allow you to consider a variety of possible solutions.**

Here then are some examples of good Design Briefs. They are concise and do not show preconceived ideas which restrict what materials may be used:

▸ Design a unit for carrying artists' materials
▸ Design a system for helping visitors to find their way round a building
▸ Design a container for carrying milk bottles
▸ Design a support for a person with a broken leg.

2.2   Analysing a problem

The next stage is to analyse a problem. The best way to begin the analysis is by making a *list* of the aspects of the problem that need to be resolved. You can then refer to these aspects one at a time. Again, stating the details concisely and clearly will help you check the points that have to be considered in the actual designing stage. It will also make it easier for an assessor or examiner to follow what you are doing. This will at least persuade him or her that your communication skills are good.

> **State the context of the specific need in your analysis.**

The analysis should refer to the *specific needs* that have to be resolved within the context given in the Design Brief. Designing a support system for a television screen in a hospital ward, or a visual display unit on a railway platform, can be quite different problems from designing a support system for a television in the home. So the *context* of the problem should be stated in the analysis, if it has not already been stated in the Design Brief.

> **The number of items produced will influence the techniques of production.**

The number of items to be made has quite an influence upon the *techniques* that will be used to produce or process the product, so state clearly how many are required.

When more than one product is required you have to consider processes used in *batch production*, e.g. casting, moulding, production lines involving a team of pupils, use of jigs, etc.

66 The aspects that might be considered for your analysis. 99

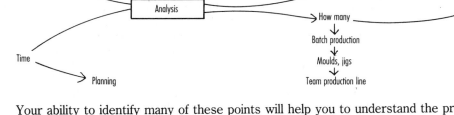

Fig 1.4
A framework for your analysis

66 Listing the aspects of your analysis has many advantages. 99

Your ability to identify many of these points will help you to understand the problem and to collect the *appropriate information* in your research. It will also help you to arrive at a *solution* that fulfils the Design Brief.

If you *list* these points as a), b), c), d), etc. you will be able to refer to them throughout the designing process to make sure that you are doing what is required. Also, in the final evaluation you will find it most helpful to go through the list and make your judgement on each specific part of the analysis. For example, if it was stated in the analysis as point c) that the solution or product must be corrosion resistant, you can answer this implied question with a 'Yes', 'Partially' or 'No' response. You might then state a *reason* for your response and, if necessary, make a recommendation for improvement.

2.3 Specification

When a detail is *specified* it usually means that it cannot be altered. For example, a specification could be that the solution must be no larger than 300mm × 150mm × 50mm. So if you design and make a solution that is just slightly larger than any of the dimensions given, it may prove to be useless because it cannot be fitted into the space required. Even if all the other design requirements are satisfactorily resolved, the solution would still be unsuitable.

2.4 Planning

Completing the project requires a number of skills, most of which depend on your personal experience, knowledge, and ability to look ahead and make calculated judgements about just how long it will take to complete a task. You may start by breaking up the total time allocated for completing the project into smaller units of time, so that you have a certain amount of time in which to complete each part of a designing process. If you calculate that the *making stage* of the artefact, system, etc. is ten weeks, then the *process of manufacture* that you choose must enable you to complete all stages of manufacture within ten weeks. If the method of manufacture that you are considering is slow, and when broken into stages takes more than ten weeks to complete, then you would be wise to select a quicker process.

66 Good planning will help you to complete your project on time. 99

Timing how long something will take has to be linked closely with your planning. The important date to work from is the *completion date*. If you work backwards from this date to the starting date, you will see what time is available. You can then develop a *planner* with a slot for each week which outlines the stages you plan to undertake in that week. Such a planner can form part of your Design Folio, and it will be evidence to the examiner of your ability to plan and organise your time.

2.5 Materials

Normally you should not have to be specific – in the analysis – about the *materials* that are to be used. You can keep in mind a material that will not corrode, if that forms part of the analysis, but the specific material should not be chosen until you have reached a more advanced stage and considered processes, time available, material availability, design features, etc.

You will find some helpful examples and comments in Chapters 3 and 4, where you can see suggestions on how to present an assignment and actual examples of students' work.

2.6 Research

Secondary research involves using someone else's work. Do acknowledge the use of such work.

Once you have completed your analysis of the problem, the next stage will involve finding out more about the problem. To show this ability, you must present *evidence* that you have searched for information. This can be done in a number of ways. Much research comes from *reading* books, magazines, catalogues, etc. Since this source of information involves someone else's research, you are required to *acknowledge* the title of the book or magazine and the name of the author, etc. This type of research is called *secondary research* and is perhaps the main source of information used in projects.

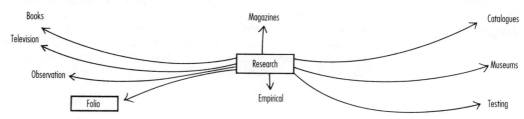

Fig 1.5
Types of research which can yield information

Primary research involves finding out for yourself.

Though secondary research takes time it is not thought of so highly as *primary research*. Primary research involves finding out for yourself; and not relying upon information gained from someone else. Sometimes the type of information you require is not available in books or magazines, so you *have* to find out for yourself anyway. For example, if you need to know how long a child plays with a red ball or a blue ball, it would be easier to devise an *experiment* to find out for yourself than to plough through a lot of reading material. The ability *to set up a sequence of experiments*, *to record your findings accurately*, and *to arrive at appropriate conclusions* from the information gathered is a highly important part of coursework. Often this helps to distinguish the more able candidate from the weaker candidate. However, do not be tempted to devise experiments just for the sake of trying to impress an assessor when information *is* readily available. For example, it is possible to find out the melting point of a range of different solders by referring to a table found in the back of most technical books. If you do plan to carry out primary research, make sure that the information is not already available. Otherwise you might waste time and possibly fail to meet the completion date for your project.

2.7 Developing ideas

This is a task that many pupils find difficult. If the analysing and the research have been done thoroughly, ideas will have been forming in your mind before these stages were completed. Remember, designing is something we all do in slightly different ways and if your method does not quite fit the description given in Fig 1.6, it may be because you have found a method that suits you better. Designing is not necessarily a sequence of logical events. Our minds tend to jump on ahead. The starting of a new stage may therefore have been *before* the completion of the previous task. This is quite normal, but it is helpful if you present the stages of your project in a logical sequence.

Try to keep an open mind and to consider a range of alternative solutions.

The ability to look at a variety of possible solutions often requires many personal qualities. Because you think you have a good idea you may wish to go straight ahead, working out a few details and then moving on quickly to the stage of making. Stopping yourself from doing this and forcing yourself to look at other alternatives as well will require a certain amount of self-discipline and patience. Keeping an open mind is not easy, particularly when a single idea seems to fit the bill. So do try to think of other possible ideas, even if at the end they only serve to show that your first idea was a good one.

The ability to *draw* is undoubtedly a valuable skill to have. It enables you to put down on paper what is in your head and it is a valuable means of communication.

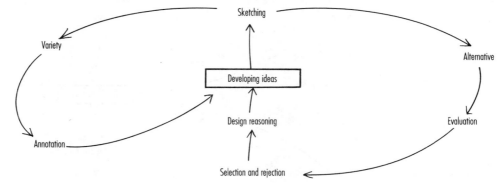

Fig 1.6
Stages involved in developing ideas

Examiners will always look to see if you have made helpful comments alongside the drawings (*annotation*). The comments may refer to weaknesses or strengths of an idea, or may compare one idea with another.

The ability to compare one idea with another and to relate them to the Design Brief and analysis is most important when *selecting* an idea for detailed development. Your ability to assess the feasibility of various ideas is going to make the difference between arriving at a solution that is suitable and one that is not suitable. The ability to *select* an idea worth carrying on with is important both for the success of your project and for the outcome of your assessment.

You will notice that the word 'evaluation' is appearing already. The act of evaluating is something that is happening throughout a design activity. It is not just reserved for that final stage which comes after the solution is made. In order to move from one detail to another you will need to make evaluative judgements about the suitability of a material, process, method of production, time allocation, etc. When decisions are made they are often the result of considering a range of advantages and disadvantages.

> 66 **Evaluation takes place throughout the design activity.** 99

2.8 Developing the chosen solution

Here you must select a suitable *means* of construction and choose the *materials* to be used in that construction. This will test your knowledge of materials, their properties and the processes by which they can be shaped, formed, joined, etc. to produce the final product. Your ability to *apply* this knowledge will be tested by the suitability of the materials and processes you have selected (Fig 1.7).

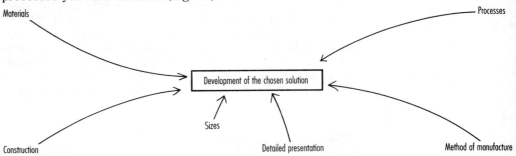

Fig 1.7
Considerations in the development of the chosen solution

Before preparing a working drawing, which is drawn to scale, you need to present an *artistic impression* of what the developed idea looks like. This often means a three-dimensional drawing of the idea, accompanied by other drawings of hidden detail to show the method of construction. There should be sufficient detail in this drawing to show the main sizes, and the specific names of the materials to be used. Your ability to draw and your knowledge of construction are being assessed in this section. One very successful method of presenting this information is through the use of exploded Isometric Projection.

2.9 The working drawing

The working drawing is a test of your ability to work out to the last detail how your design solution is to be made and your ability to present the information accurately and clearly. Most working drawings are presented in two-dimensional drawings using Orthographic Projection and standards recommended by the British Standards Institution (BSI) in their publication PP 7308.

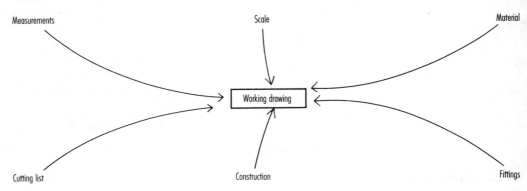

Fig 1.8
Aspects of a working drawing

In this section you are being tested on your ability to present information clearly *and* on your knowledge and understanding of how to use BSI recommendations. You should be familiar with such conventions as drawing hidden detail, sections, dimensions, scales, cutting lists, etc. and you must be able to apply them appropriately. Besides being able to draw according to BSI recommendations, you will be expected to know the difference between First Angle and Third Angle Projection (see p. 34).

Not all working drawings have to be in Orthographic Projection. For example, it would be difficult and of no advantage to use this method in drawing *natural forms*, such as those which might be produced in pottery, beaten metal, jewellery, sculpture, etc. But there should still be sufficient detail to show *how* the final product is to be made. These drawings can also be supported with *models* made in clay or plasticine. But it is important that they should be made to *scale*, so that the true proportions of height, width, etc. can be shown.

2.10   Making skills

Making skills can, of course, be quite wide ranging. Though the three main materials used in CDT are wood, metal and plastics, other materials such as clay, concrete, card, glass, etc. are not excluded. So you will need to develop the skills required to mould, shape, bend and join these materials in the correct and safe manner.

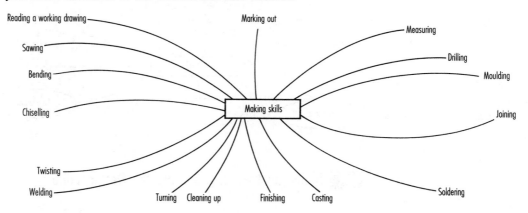

Fig 1.9
The various making skills

If you allow the solution to dictate the materials to be used and the shapes to be achieved, you may find yourself having to learn new techniques, skills and processes. This of course is a very good reason for learning new skills. But you have to take into account *how long* it will take you to acquire these skills. Will you be able to acquire the skills *and* complete the making in the time available? It may therefore be sensible to select a shape or form that takes into consideration *your own* experience and ability, so that you are sure of completing a project. It is much wiser to demonstrate what you *can* do well, than to select a new area of learning in which you are unsure that you will master the skills involved. Think carefully about this when developing your chosen idea. The assessor of the *practical solution* will be looking at how well everything fits together, how well it functions, the quality of finish, and the overall quality of appearance. (The assessor will not be concerned with such quality in terms of the *design solution*, since this will already have been assessed in the Design Folio.)

> **Think of your own skills when selecting particular materials and techniques.**

2.11   Evaluation

The evaluation is your judgement of how well the solution fulfils the Design Brief. Though you may arrive at a decision that it *does* do what is required, you have to analyse how well it fulfils not only the Design Brief but also the analysis and specifications if given.

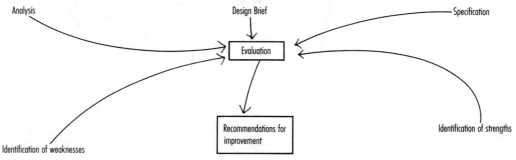

Fig 1.10
Aspects of evaluation

RECOMMENDATIONS FOR IMPROVEMENT

The final stage is to recommend areas that need to be improved and to suggest how such improvements could be made. The improvements can relate to methods of production and choice of materials, as well as to design features such as proportion, colour, finish, etc.

So far the main skills have been outlined for a single project. You may find that you are required to do more than one project during your course. If so, the same skills will be assessed in both projects.

UNIT 3   DESIGN FOLIO

The Design Folio is an important document and it is the record and evidence of the work you have done. It is advisable to keep a separate folio for each project. Besides the skills already outlined, it is necessary to give some thought to the skills that are required to produce a folio.

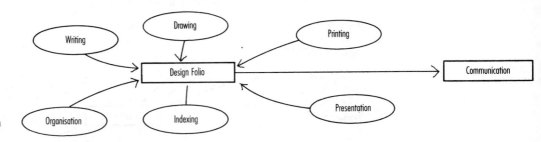

Fig 1.11
Skills involved in producing the Design Folio

3.1   Skills involved in producing the Design Folio

DRAWING

Drawing has already been discussed as a skill used in the recording of information and in the development of ideas. So the Design Folio should provide simple evidence of your ability to use a variety of drawing techniques. However, you may feel that you could extend your drawing skills to include the *cover* for the Folio. While there is not a specific mark allocated for the cover it does help to create a good impression. Remember, it is often the cover of a book that makes you want to look inside.

Fig 1.12
Examples of Design Folio cover

ORGANISATION

The organisation of a folio is concerned with the arrangement of the sheets or pages and their placing in a logical order. It is important to *number* the sheets and give them a *title*, e.g. Design Brief, Analysis, Research, Development of Ideas, Development of Chosen Idea, Working Drawing, Evaluation. These seven sections can be thought of as chapters and each chapter may have several pages. A *contents list*, together with page numbers, will help the reader to use the information you have presented and will be evidence of your ability to organise.

PRINTING

Printing can cover a range of calligraphy skills, and if you happen to present written information using a style that is pleasing to look at, as well as being easy to read, so much the better. But *time* is important, so do not use a style that takes a lot of your time. You can, of course, also use letter-press techniques, lettering stencils, word processors, etc. Although the skills needed to use these techniques are different from those needed for calligraphy, they can be demonstrated in the way you present your Folio. The Folio must communicate clearly your thinking and the development of your project, and it is this that is really being assessed.

3.2 Summary of skills assessed in coursework

Coursework is a way of assessing your ability to:

▶ identify a need
▶ write a Design Brief
▶ write an analysis
▶ gather, store and organise research information
▶ develop ideas
▶ develop a chosen idea
▶ produce a Working Drawing
▶ make a design solution
▶ evaluate
▶ present your coursework as a complete package.

Presentation of coursework does play an important part in your assessment and some care and thought should be given to this final stage. You could simply put your completed Design Folio and completed product or system on a table and leave it for assessment. If, however, the table top is covered with a sheet of coloured paper and a few sheets from the folio are displayed on a vertical surface this will help you to present your coursework as a package (see p.31).

UNIT 4   COURSEWORK REQUIREMENTS OF EACH EXAMINING GROUP

Though what has been outlined above as the requirements for coursework is common to all the Examining Groups, there are slight variations as to how and when coursework should be done and presented.

4.1 London and East Anglian Group (LEAG)

All candidates must submit coursework and great importance is attached to this element of the assessment scheme. The teacher is the best person to judge the total contribution each candidate has made in this area. The coursework will be internally assessed and externally moderated in accordance with the scheme prepared and issued by the Group.

What this means is that *you* have to do the coursework in this subject. It will first be assessed by your teacher, and then the marks given by your teacher will be adjusted, if necessary, to match with the agreed standard set by the Examining Group. This is so that the standards are the same in every school or college.

The submission should be a representative selection of work normally undertaken during the last two years of the course. The selection should be made by the candidate. It must include designs and artefacts and show that the candidate has obtained expertise in ONE material and experience in at least ONE other. Teachers may advise candidates on the selection of appropriate coursework.

Though all coursework is assessed in the first stage by your *teacher*, you do not have to display all your coursework for a *visiting assessor*. So you can obviously pick your best work, so long as it shows that you have a working experience in more than one material. It is desirable for you to show a complete package, i.e. a Design Folio and a related piece of practical work. But it is possible for you to show your best Folio along with your best piece of practical work, and the two need not be part of the same project.

The allocation of marks for coursework will be as follows:

Designing	30 marks
Planning	10 marks
Making	50 marks
Evaluation	10 marks
TOTAL	100 marks

The point to notice here is that the work you show in the Design Folio (designing, planning and evaluation) is worth the same as the product you make. In other words, they are of equal importance and value.

ASSESSMENT OF COURSEWORK

Coursework will consist of evidence of design work and of realisation. Some design work will not lead to artefacts being made and some practical work will not necessarily be the product of a candidate's own design activity. However, it is expected that substantial evidence of related design and realisation will be presented by the candidate. The emphasis should show that the candidate has been involved in design and realisation as an integrated process.

What this is telling you is that you can show a Design Folio for a piece of work that was never made and that you can show a piece of practical work that had already been designed. This is, of course, providing that you do show an example of a complete design and make project.

Although normally the coursework will be an individual-based activity, a group approach to design and realisation is not excluded. In order to assess group coursework, the contribution of each candidate must be clearly identifiable.

In other words, you can be a member of a *team* to design and make a product, so long as the part *you* were responsible for can be identified and assessed.

Research investigations, which form part of the 'problem solving' process, are a necessary element of a realisation project and evidence of this research should be submitted. Technology and theory notes which form part of the learning process are not required for coursework assessment.

In other words, keep all *evidence* of research such as letters, magazines, manufacturers' literature, etc. even if it was too bulky to place in your Design Folio. Note books on materials, processes, tools, etc. are not needed for assessment.

Fig 1.13 gives a breakdown of how the marks are distributed and how many marks are required to fit a category from unsatisfactory to superb.

Category		Design	Planning	Making	Evaluation
Outstanding	Superb	25–30	9–10	41–50	9–10
Above average	Highly satisfactory	19–24	7–8	31–40	7–8
Average	Satisfactory	13–18	5–6	21–30	5–6
Below average	Slightly unsatisfactory	7–12	3–4	11–20	3–4
Weak	Unsatisfactory	0–6	0–2	0–10	0–2

Fig 1.13
Mark distribution

Outstanding candidate

To help you to have an idea of what a candidate has to do to achieve an outstanding mark here is a description of what is expected.

A student who fits this description is a likely A grade candidate.

Design   Understands and analyses a brief. Thoroughly researches and investigates the problem. Generates a wide range of proposals. Makes well-reasoned decisions. Produces clear and comprehensive drawings.

Planning   Prepares a logical and realistic plan, correctly detailing materials, tools and operations needed to produce an artefact to a defined standard and within all relevant constraints.

Making   Uses tools safely and correctly, with skill and sensitivity. Works confidently and accurately, produces a good finish. Adapts to changing circumstances.

Evaluating   Carries out a full and critical appraisal of the product. Accurately identifies and describes its strengths and weaknesses. Offers proposals for its improvement.

Average candidate

A similar method is used to describe what is expected of an average candidate.

Design   Identifies the essential features of a design task. Produces some evidence of research and investigation. Settles on a solution often based on a known form of procedures. Produces understandable sketches covering major details.

Planning   Plans the major stages of a scheme, which usually needs modification to match available tools, materials, costs and time.

Making   With some supervision produces work within specified requirements. The quality of the work is usually adequate but quality may be sacrificed to achieve completeness.

Evaluating   Compares product with design brief. Shows awareness of function, aesthetics and cost but rarely makes detached and unbiased judgements.

Weak candidate

Finally the Examining Group has described what is expected of a weak candidate.

Designing   Depends on questions and suggestions from the teacher to generate at least one solution to a design problem although response may not always be appropriate. Reproduces conventional ideas. Drawings produced need explanations.

Planning   Can list the steps required to execute a familiar task. Able to detail individual steps within a longer term plan produced by the teacher.

Making   Given supervision, assistance, time and encouragement, can follow an instruction sheet and produce an acceptable end product, although not always at the first attempt.

Evaluating   Has difficulty in accepting the need for an evaluation stage. Has a disproportionate concern with functional aspects in terms of success and failure.

As you can see from this last description, even a weak candidate is expected to do something in *every part* of the stages of designing to be considered for a grade. The last description would possibly fit a grade G candidate, possibly bordering on the grade F. That is, of course, providing that the other elements of the course (i.e. the Technology examination and the Design and Realisation paper) have been completed. Remember that for this Examining Group the coursework element has a value of 40%.

4.2 Midland Examining Group (MEG)

Coursework is worth 30% of the total marks. It follows the common pattern of solving a problem through designing and making. MEG also requires candidates to be experienced in more than one material. However, towards the end of the course, work may be produced in a single material if appropriate.

The weighting of the marks for coursework is as follows:

1	Identification, analysis and investigation	15 marks
2	Generation and development of ideas	25 marks
3	Realisation of design solution	46 marks
4	Evaluation of their own design solutions	10 marks
5	Safety	4 marks
		TOTAL 100 marks

Again you will notice that the *designing* skills and the *making* skills (items 1, 2 and 4) add up to 50%. The 4% for *safety* is added to the *realisation* of design since it is during the making that safe handling of tools, machines, etc. is so important.

The table shown on p. 41–2 indicates what you are expected to do to get high, medium, or low marks, and can be compared with the other tables given in this book. Though different words are used, such tables are very similar from one Examining Group to another.

4.3 Northern Examining Association (NEA)

NEA does not have a Design and Realisation paper of the type used by LEAG and MEG. It therefore allocates a full 50% of available marks to coursework.

> Candidates will be required to submit for assessment a project which has been carried out in the twelve calendar months preceding the written examination.

Since the examinations mainly fall in June this means that the coursework should be done in the final term of your fourth year and in the first two terms of your fifth year at school.

> Each project must consist of a design folio and the corresponding realisation.

So, unlike LEAG, NEA does not allow unrelated design and practical work to be submitted for coursework. However, candidates only submit work completed during the twelve calendar months preceding the written examination.

> Candidates may opt to produce only one large project or several smaller ones, but in either case the equivalent of at least two full terms' work will be expected.
> The format of the Design Folio should clearly reflect the scheme of assessment and be fastened together in a logical sequence.

The mark allocation below indicates the format the Design Folio should take and the order in which the elements of designing should be presented.

Mark allocation

Design skills 25%	Research	5
	Analysis	7
	Synthesis	20
	Final Evaluation	8
	Visual Communication	10
	TOTAL	50
Manufacturing skills 25%	Construction Quality	25
	Accuracy	10
	Finish	10
	Appearance	5
	TOTAL	50

Marks will be awarded as follows:

Identification of a problem (this is the same as a 'need')	10
Analysis, investigation, and initial ideas	20
Development of chosen ideas	20
Quality of graphic communication, including working drawings	20
Evaluation	10
TOTAL	80

You will find that all the elements of designing have been allocated marks, but some of the terms used are different from those used by the other Examining Groups. For example, Synthesis, Final Evaluation, Visual Communication and Constructional Quality are used. **Synthesis** means bringing information and ideas together in order to produce a single solution. So under the heading of Synthesis come the terms commonly used by the other Examining Groups such as development of ideas, development of a chosen idea, and production of a Working Drawing.

4.4 Southern Examining Group (SEG)

SEG allocates 50% of the total marks to coursework. You can do one major project or two or three smaller projects. Whichever you choose to do you must show a wide range of knowledge, skill and experience. There are more marks available for the making than for the designing, i.e. 30% for the making but only 20% for designing.

The assessment of the Design Folio follows the pattern that is commonly used by the Examining Groups.

Identification of a problem (this is the same as a 'need')	10
Analysis, investigation, and initial ideas	20
Development of chosen idea	20
Quality of graphic communication, including working drawing	20
Evaluation	10

TOTAL 80

The assessment for the *making* part of the coursework is marked out of 120. This then gives the balance of 10% more marks for the making skills than for the designing skills in the Design Folio (120 marks to 80 marks is the same ratio as 30% to 20%).

All work that is done during the course is assessed by your teacher, but only *one* artefact need be submitted for your final assessment if it clearly shows your ability.

Coursework requirements

Work presented for assessment will, normally, be work undertaken in the final year of the course. Work done in the previous year may be submitted but the standards by which the work will be assessed will be the standards that a candidate in the final year of the course could be expected to achieve.

The work that each candidate should have available for assessment and moderation is as follow:
  i) one artefact which, in the opinion of the teacher, best fulfils the assessment objectives of the syllabus and indicates the abilities of the candidate;
  ii) the Design Folio in support of the artefact selected.

Assessment of coursework – practical

The realisation of the design is marked solely for the quality of making skills and the assessment does not take into consideration any aspect of the work recorded in the Design Folio.

Band 7	A product with very little evidence of adequate workmanship. The work will usually be incomplete and therefore will not fulfil its function. Surface finish not considered.	1–18
Band 6	A product that is just adequate to fulfil functional or aesthetic requirements but lacks any refinement. Little attention given to the selection, preparation, and application of a suitable finish, resulting in an unattractive appearance.	19–35
Band 5	A product well enough made to fulfil its functional or aesthetic requirements but limited to manipulative skills resulting in some obvious constructional shortcomings. A suitable surface finish will have been applied but with some blemishes evident.	36–52
Band 4	An adequate overall standard of workmanship but with aspects of the product indicating a lack of manipulative skills, leading to difficulties with constructional operations. The quality of manufacture is sufficient to enable the product to fulfil its function. Surface finishes will have been adequately applied.	53–69
Band 3	A good standard of workmanship with sound construction in the materials used. Individual components will fit together well, with only small inaccuracies. Surface finishes will be sufficiently well applied to produce a good appearance.	70–86

Band 2	A high standard of workmanship with some refinement in shaping materials and in the production and fitting of parts. Surface finishes will be, generally, very good but with minor faults usually in difficult places.	87–103
Band 1	A very high level of workmanship showing refinement and accuracy in shaping materials and a high degree of skill in the production and fitting of parts. Surface finish will be of a type and quality ideally suited to functional and aesthetic considerations. Applied finishes will, generally, be blemish free.	104–120

4.5 Northern Ireland Schools Examinations Council (NISEC)

NISEC allocates 50% of the marks to coursework. All the designing and making done during the two-year course is assessed by your teacher. The Examining Group, however, also sets six Design Briefs from which you must select one to be completed in your normal lesson and homework time. The Design Briefs are set at different levels of difficulty and it is sensible for you to choose one that will enable you to complete what is required.

4.6 Welsh Joint Education Committee (WJEC)

WJEC allocates 50% of the marks to coursework. This is then equally divided between the designing and the making of your project. The work is first of all assessed by your teacher and then by a visiting moderator.

Coursework in this syllabus comes under the heading *Design Study*. This is because the Examining Group sets five design topics from which you must choose one. If, however, you wish to choose a topic of your own you may do so. The ones set by the Examining Group should then be used as a guide, so that your chosen topic involves similar tasks of Identification of a Need, Investigation, Writing a Design Brief, etc. You will receive the details of the topics early in the course so that you can start your Design Study during the fourth year. It is intended that you should have a period of not less than one year before the date of the written examinations to complete your design study.

4.7 International General Certificate of Secondary Education (IGCSE)

IGCSE is a course designed for students not living in the UK. It is prepared and examined by the University of Cambridge Local Examinations Syndicate.

The course is divided into a *core*, which all candidates do, and an *extended* area of study. This is called a 'Supplement' and is available for candidates who want to get an A or B grade. The candidates who take the Core only can achieve grades between C and G; candidates who take the Core plus the Supplement can get grades between A and E. The Core includes a project that is taken during the final two terms of the course. The Examining Group sets a thematic topic and candidates are required to prepare a Design Brief.

4.8 Summary

All the courses require coursework even though the terms used to describe this may vary. Most of the courses give a weighting of 50% of the total marks to coursework-type activities. Three examining groups set *themes* or topics, i.e. MEG, WJEC and IGCSE, but WJEC also give you an open choice. The time allocated to coursework varies from five terms to two terms. All coursework must be available for assessment, except that for LEAG, where a *selection* can be made available. All work, no matter how many projects have been attempted, is marked *as a whole*. All coursework is assessed by the teacher and moderated by a representative of the examining body.

RESEARCHING A TOPIC

There are two areas of research. The first is in the *identification of a need*, and the second is in finding the *relevant materials* for fulfilling that need.

As you will have seen in Chapter 1, some of the Examining Groups set topics or themes, though others leave you to make a free choice. Here we start by dealing with the situation where you have some choice in the theme or topic selected.

UNIT 1   CHOOSING A THEME OR TOPIC FOR COURSEWORK

In Chapter 1 there was a brief discussion about identifying a need. Most problem-solving activities start from the identification of a need, so it is here that *you* should begin when seeking to choose a topic.

If you are not certain about a topic, then start by writing the word 'need' in the middle of a blank sheet of A4 paper. Around that word write the main areas or activities that you are involved in and just put them down as they come into your head. It is not important at this stage whether or not they mean a lot to you. Just leave your mind open to any possibility. Fig 1.2 on p. 2 shows you four main areas surrounding the starting point: home, society, school and leisure. You can add to these by putting down other main areas, such as transport, appearance, protection, storing, etc. With this web of eight main areas, you may now be able to branch out from one or more of the main areas to see if it will lead you nearer to finding a specific topic for study. The web may now begin to look something like Fig 2.1.

> **By branching out from your starting point you can develop a web of ideas. This will help you focus on a specific topic.**

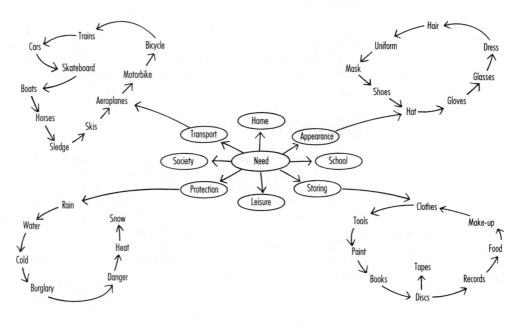

Fig 2.1
Web of ideas

You do not have to expand on all the main areas; and you only continue adding to the web for as long as it takes to help you identify a need. For instance, from 'Need' at the centre of the web go to one of the main areas, say 'Protection', and then select a word from the next branch, e.g. 'Burglary'. You are now beginning to *link* words that should help you to direct your attention towards a specific need. In this example you may find the need to have an alarm system for a car, bicycle, cupboard, desk, etc. The specific need could now be perhaps identified as *an anti-theft device for your bicycle*.

Another way of finding needs is to *ask questions*. There are large groups of people in such places as schools, hospitals, stations, sports grounds, homes for the elderly, shopping centres, gymnasiums, parks, etc. You might visit such a location or write to someone who is in charge. If you decide to make initial contact by writing a letter, you are strongly advised to get assistance from your teacher. Though he or she will not be expected to compose the letter, they will be able to advise you what to write and how it should be presented. In any case, if you used school headed paper it is possible that you will need the permission of the head teacher. Many students do communicate with local industry and commerce using school headed notepaper, but the letter is always typed and looked at by a senior teacher before it is posted.

Asking people questions may help you identify what they regard as a 'need' and this may give you ideas for your project.

Looking at past students' projects is another way of helping to identify a need. You may be attracted first by the solution, but it will help if you read back to the Design Brief and to some early statement of the 'need' which lay behind the project.

▶ UNIT 2 SOURCES OF INFORMATION

Wherever information is *stored*, there is a possible source of information.

2.1 Books

> ❝ **Books are still the most widely used source of information.** ❞

Books are possibly the most widely used source of information. There is a skill in using books efficiently. Most often you only need small bits of information. So you first of all select a book by its *title*, then look at the *table of contents* to see if the information is covered. Or you look in the *index* at the back to see if the word or name you require to know something about is listed. Against the word will be page numbers. Turn to those pages to see what information is given on that item. When you do find something, make a *note* of the title of the book and the page number straight away, because you may need to refer to that text again at a later date. If the information is brief you can write down a few notes and/or sketches of diagrams etc. If, however, there is quite a lot of relevant information you may save time by having it photocopied. But check the photocopying regulations with your teacher or librarian first.

2.2 Magazines

Magazines are often an excellent source of up-to-date information. This is because most magazines are compiled on a weekly or monthly basis. Books take much longer to write and be printed, and are not usually revised and brought up-to-date every year. The contents of magazines are often listed on the cover, with more detail on contents given on the first few pages.

2.3 Catalogues

> ❝ **Specialist catalogues are a useful source of specific, up-to-date information.** ❞

Often some very reliable information can be obtained from specialist catalogues. You can gain information about sizes, quantities, function, materials, etc. and also on costs. To know the cost of, say, some small DC 5V motor may be the deciding factor in the selection of an energy source for a project. Catalogues can be obtained in shops or by filling in a form that is part of an advertisement and posting it to the address given. Remember that you may have to enclose money or stamps for the catalogue to be sent to you.

Mail order catalogues are readily available in most homes and form an easy way of obtaining information. There is a danger, however, that some students will find it so easy that they will do little more to gain information.

The advantage of gaining information from catalogues is that the selected material can be cut out with a pair of scissors and pasted in a Research Folio. But do remember that it is not how much you collect that is important, but how *selective* you are in extracting relevant information for your project.

2.4 Dictionaries and encyclopaedias

These are often helpful in finding information which will be a starting point. The dictionaries tend to give a briefer explanation than the encyclopaedias and make less use of illustrations.

The Longman *GCSE Reference Guides* are specially prepared for GCSE students and there is one available for CDT. This Reference Guide provides brief but detailed information and makes considerable use of illustration.

2.5 Libraries

You should start by looking for information in the school or college library because most of the books kept there have been selected by teachers who are aware of your needs. They will not only have selected them for their subject matter, but also for the level that is appropriate.

You should be familiar with knowing how to find the books that you think you need. If you already know the *title*, you can look in the *alphabetical title file* and see if the book is kept in that library. If you find a card you will see a *number*. The first three digits of that number will tell you the section, e.g. 400 tells you that the section is Languages, 500 is Pure Science, 600 is Technology (applied science), 700 the Arts, and so on. Within these main groups are ten sub-groups, e.g. within Technology is 610 Medical Science, 620 Engineering, 630 Agriculture, 640 Domestic Arts and Sciences, 650 Business, 660 Chemical Technology, 670 Manufactures, 680 Assembled Products, 690 Buildings. This helps you to *narrow down* the section of the library relevant to your project. There are even more subdivisions which you should become familiar with so that you can concentrate on just a few shelves.

> **Learn how to use the library classification.**

The books are placed in numerical order so that it is easy to see if the book you want is on the shelf. If there is a break in the sequence of numbers then it is possible that the book you want is on loan. The librarian has a list of books on loan and can confirm whether this is so. If the book you want is important, you can fill out a reservation card so that as soon as it is returned you will be told. If the library has not got the books you require, you can still fill in a card so that the library can order the books from other libraries. Several weeks may pass before they can get the book, so do give the librarian as much notice as possible.

2.6 Museums

Museums are an excellent source of information, though you may think that museums are just places where things of the past are stored. Many museums are housed in large buildings, but there are also outdoor museums called open-air museums. These are often *active* museums where many of the exhibits are made to move, especially in the industrial museums where, for example, an engine is brought to life, a candle-making shop produces candles, the machine print shop prints newspapers, signs, etc. The production of these and many other items of the past is demonstrated in the original buildings so that you can see the conditions in which your grandparents and their parents worked. Well-known examples of open-air museums are the Ironbridge Gorge Museum or the Beamish Museum in Durham. However, if you want to find out more, here are the addresses of Area Museums. They specialise in helping pupils who are taking GCSE and they help other museums in their area to do all they can to help students in their coursework studies. There may be one near you.

> **Museums can be an invaluable source of information.**

▶ Yorkshire and Humberside Museums Council, Farnley Hall, Hall Lane, Leeds LS12 5HA
▶ Area Museum Council for the South West, Hestercombe House, Cheddon, Fitzpain, Taunton TA2 8LQ
▶ Area Museums Service for South Eastern England, Ferroners House, Barbican, London EC2Y 8AA
▶ The Council of Museums in Wales, 32 Park Place, Cardiff CF1 3BA
▶ East Midlands Area Museums Service, Courtyard Buildings, Walloton Park, Nottingham NG8 2A8
▶ North of England Museums Service, 27 Sutton Street, Durham DH1 4BW
▶ North West Museum and Art Gallery Service, Griffin Lodge, Griffin Park, Blackburn BB2 2PN
▶ West Midlands Area Museum Service, Avoncroft Museum of Buildings, Stoke Prior, Bromsgrove, Worcs B60 4JR

Here are some other addresses of museums that are concerned with educational use and which may also be able to advise you about resources for your course.

▶ **Northern Ireland**: Ulster Folk and Transport Museum, Cultra Manor, Holywood, Belfast BT18 0EU
▶ **Midlands**: Castle Museum and Art Gallery, Castle Road, Nottingham NG2 6EL
▶ **North West**: Bolton Museum and Art Gallery, Le Mans Crescent, Bolton, Lancs BL1 1SA
▶ **South West/Wales**: Royal Albert Memorial Museum, Queen Street, Exeter, EX4 3RX

▶ **London:** Geffrye Museum, Kingsland Road, London E2 8EA
▶ **North:** Louise Wheatley, 11 New Walk Terrace, Fishergate, York YO1 4BG
▶ **South East:** Portsmouth City Museum and Art Gallery, Museum Road, Portsmouth PO1 2LJ
▶ **Scotland:** Glasgow Art Gallery and Museum, Kelvingrove, Glasgow G3 8AG

Before contacting these services you should check with your teacher just in case a visit may already have been arranged.

2.7 Observation

The things and the people around you are an instant source of information. Although everything you see is going to be an endless source, you do need to *direct* your observation on a topic. So, if your concern is finding out something about *transport*, then concentrate on just that. Remember, you are wanting to observe *and* to collect information. So make good use of sketching in a sketch pad, and try to annotate (add notes to) your sketches. If you are using a pen or pencil, the sketch will be in black (or blue) and white so you may need to add a note about the colour or type of material of the object you have drawn. Any information which does not show up in the drawing can always be added in brief notes.

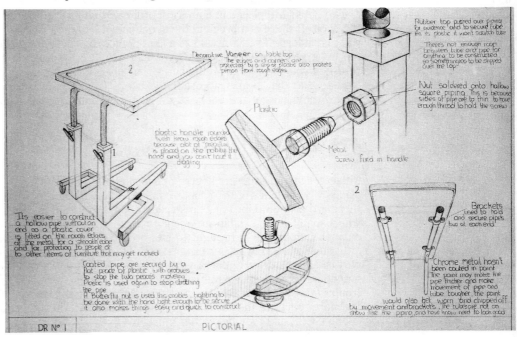

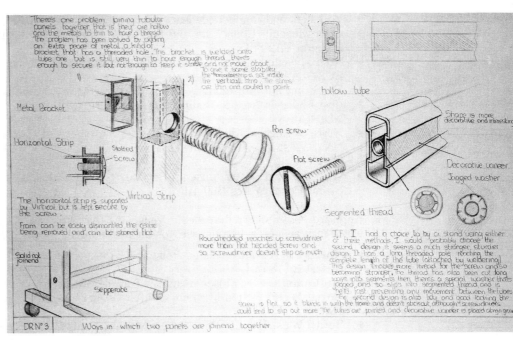

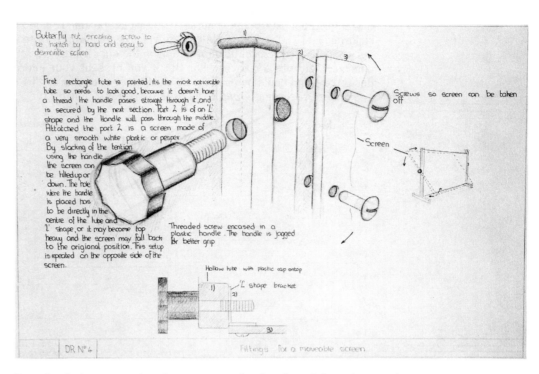

Butterfly nut encasing screw to be tighten by hand and easy to dismantle screen

First rectangle tube is pointed, its the most noticeable tube so needs to look good, because it doesn't have a thread the handle passes straight through it, and is secured by the next section. Part 2 is of an 'L' shape and the Handle will pass through the middle. Attached the part 2 is a screen made of a very smooth white plastic or pespex. By slacking of the tention using the handle the screen can be tilted up or down. The hole where the handle is placed has to be directly in the centre of the tube and 'L' shape, or it may become top heavy and the screen may fall back to the original position. This setup is repeated on the opposite side of the screen.

Screws so screen can be taken off

Screen

Threaded screw encased in a plastic handle. The handle is jagged for better grip

Hollow tube with plastic cap ontop

'L' shape bracket

DR N° 4   Fittings for a moveable screen

Fig 2.2
Examples of annotated exploded drawing

Drawing helps you to be observant, so do sketch and draw items whenever you can.

OBSERVING PEOPLE

> **The best source of information is often direct observation.**

This can include observation of the very young to the very old. If the topic of your project is concerned with young children at play, then the best resource is watching the behaviour of children at first hand. You may have to search for ages in books for information and then not be able to find exactly what you need. Instead you could go to a nursery, play group, etc., taking with you a *plan* of what you want to find out so that you make good use of your time there. List the types of detail that you need to know, e.g.:

▶ What types of things interest the children most?
▶ Does one colour seem to be more popular than another?
▶ Are boys' and girls' interests similar or different?

Having decided what you want to find out, think of ways of establishing the information you want to know. If the children are old enough you may find out some information by *asking them questions*. Formulate the questions before doing your research, so that you can put identical questions to a number of children.

2.8   Questionnaires

> **Taking samples of items with you may help overcome any confusion over words or terms.**

A carefully planned questionnaire, with a selection of answers so that only a tick in a box is required for each question, may help to speed up the task and to provide you with data that can be easily analysed. For example, suppose you wanted to find out the colour that most attracts children between the ages of 3 and 5 years. Some children may not know the names of colours and they may not be able to discriminate between, say, orange and brown, or red and pink, etc. So it would be more reliable if you took a *sample* of colours with you. Then, even if the answering is done by pointing, you will be sure that the colour you are enquiring about is the same as the one the child can see. The layout of a possible questionnaire for finding useful information is given below.

	R	Y	B	G	O	M
Question 1 Which is your favourite colour?		✓				
Question 2 Which colour do you like next best?					✓	
Question 3 Which colour do you like least?						✓

Key Red, Y = Yellow, B = Blue,
G = Green, O = Orange,
M = Mauve.

If you visited a playgroup or nursery you would be able to find out the responses of, say, 20 children, and you would begin to see which were the favourite colours and which were not very popular. To *record* the information on the questionnaire as shown above, you would need one questionnaire for each child. But if you present your information differently you could design one that could be used for 20 children or even more. The example shown below is just one way of recording *group* responses (here for 27 children).

Favourite colour

		Children's reponse																		
	1	2	3	4	5	6	7	8	9	10	11	12	13	14	15	16	17	18	19	20
Red	x	x	x	x	x	x	x	x	x											
Yellow	x	x	x	x	x	x	x	x	x	x	x	x	x							
Blue	x																			
Green	x																			
Orange	x	x	x	x																
Mauve																				

Next favourite colour

	1	2	3	4	5	6	7	8	9	10	11	12	13	14	15	16	17	18	19	20
Red																				
Yellow																				
Blue	x	x	x	x	x	x	x													
Green	x	x	x	x	x	x	x	x	x											
Orange	x	x	x	x	x	x	x	x	x	x	x	x	x	x						
Mauve																				

Least favourite colour

	1	2	3	4	5	6	7	8	9	10	11	12	13	14	15	16	17	18	19	20
Red																				
Yellow																				
Blue	x	x	x	x	x	x	x	x	x											
Green																				
Orange																				
Mauve	x	x	x	x	x	x	x	x	x	x	x	x	x	x	x	x	x	x	x	x

Colour questionnaire: children aged 3–5 years

By shading in the squares for each response you will produce a *bar chart* that is easy to analyse at a glance. Such a questionnaire will, when completed, form a valuable source of information and part of a Design Folio.

The example given above shows only a narrow area of information related to colour and is only intended to show you how to design a questionnaire. You could put down anything that you want to find out on the left hand side and include as many responses as you think suitable for your research.

Information obtained in this way can only be reliable when a *lot* of responses are recorded. So if you feel that you have the time, and the information you are seeking is important enough, you can use the same style of chart as given above and each box can represent, say, *five* responses. This can be done by using a 'five-bar gate'. All this means is that you put a short vertical line in the one box every time you have a response. When you have five responses in that box, the last one is marked with a diagonal line going through the four vertical lines so that it looks like a five-bar gate. Then you start in the next box alongside, and so on, as shown in the example below.

> **The greater the number of responses, the more reliable the information.**

Example of a five-bar gate

Sometimes you need to find out information from much older children, or even from adults, and to help you put a *value* on the information you can use a *storing method*, based on a range of 1 to 5 or 1 to 10. A range of 1 to 10 is commonly used and most people can express a value of so many out of 10. You could design a chart with the details you want to know on the left, and the values on the right. For example, you may want to know how people rate the design of a product such as a hand torch. You would first list the information you wish to know, so you might begin your list with:

▶ Is it easy to hold?
▶ Can you switch it on and off easily?
▶ Is it easy to change the battery?
▶ Do you think it looks attractive?
▶ Does it provide enough light?
▶ How do you rate it overall?

To record the responses to these questions your questionnaire may look like the one illustrated below.

Questionnaire: Torch A

Number interviewed: 4

					Rating						
	0	1	2	3	4	5	6	7	8	9	10
Holding				✓✓	✓	✓					
Switching			✓	✓	✓	✓					
Change battery						✓	✓	✓✓			
Attractive							✓	✓	✓		✓
Lighting						✓	✓✓	✓			
Overall rating							✓✓	✓✓			

If you have *several* torches you can label them A, B, C, etc., and establish a number of facts. You could find out which torch received the highest or lowest rating. You could also discover which torch gave the best light, was the most attractive, was the easiest to operate, etc. You would most likely find that the torch that was the easiest to operate was *not* the one that appealed the most. So you could analyse the questionnaire quite deeply. Then, if your task was to design a lighting device for holding in the hand, you might incorporate the good points of each torch into a *single design*.

The findings that you get from such investigation techniques are helpful, but it must be remembered that they are not conclusive. Your findings must be regarded as a *sample of opinion* and it is up to *you* how much value you place on the findings. However, always put all the investigations you have conducted in your Research Folio. A well-thought-out questionnaire will help to establish the information you are seeking and, just as important, will help to *show* the assessor or examiner that you have done your preparation thoroughly.

2.9 Empirical research

This is not so frightening as it may at first sound. In fact empirical research is one of the simplest ways of finding out information and one that is commonly used. All it means is finding out by experiment or by trial and error. Suppose you want to know what type of *finish* will look pleasing for a wall fitting that has to go in a certain room. What better way is there of finding out than by placing a variety of *sample finishes* in the room? You can then choose the one that you like the best.

Trial and error can yield useful information.

You may wish to find out what *proportions* look pleasing for a storage unit. One good way of finding out is to get a number of pieces of spare material and to lay them out on the floor. Then you can move them and adjust them until you are satisfied that you have got the proportions that please you. You can, of course, get the opinion of other pupils and/or your teachers if you wish. Once you have decided on the final proportions, you can take the measurements down and draw them out to scale later.

It is often a good idea to *photograph* this type of empirical research so that you can present it in your Design Folio.

2.10 Models

You can find out a lot of information from 'mock ups' or models. You can see how mechanical parts move or what a design looks like in three dimensions. So if, say, there is a link mechanism that needs lengthening, you can make the arm or beam longer until you get the exact movement that you require.

Models are usually made from easily worked materials so that they can be produced quickly. Some care needs to be taken with measurements, but craftmanship is not important. Remember that you are establishing principles of function and proportion, and are not making a final product. You are most likely to work with stiff card, balsa wood, sheet material from containers such as washing up liquid bottles, metal cans, etc.

2.11 Construction kits

Using construction kits is a good way of finding out information. They can be quickly assembled and rearranged until the functioning principles have been established. They can be used again and again and there is no waste material. There are many construction kits on the market and many are used by CDT students in schools. Kits are available in shops or from such suppliers as: Economatics (Education) Ltd, Epic House, Orgreave Road, Handsworth, Sheffield.

Kits are available for specialised projects that involve mechanisms, electronics, pneumatics, hydraulics, etc. You may be familiar with such names as Lego, Meccano, or Fischertechnik. You may even have had the opportunity of using these kits.

Fig 2.3

EXAMPLES OF KITS IN USE

If you are able to establish an arrangement of parts that functions well for your needs, it is important that you make a *sketch* and *notes* of what you have developed so that you can either continue your development a stage further or incorporate what you have learnt in the design of your solution. *Photographing* the construction is a good way of recording the information and, of course, this can be used as *evidence* of your research into the problem. Some information may not appear clearly on a photograph, e.g. the number of teeth on gear wheels, so make a note of such information.

2.12 Exhibitions

To attract the public's interest exhibitions are held. Entrance is usually free and there is often free literature available. Trade exhibitions are particularly good places to visit. Here you will be able to see various materials and equipment on display and, in many cases, to obtain free samples of materials, pens, colouring pencils, and plenty of literature. Every year there is a

Craft Design and Technology Exhibition. It was at one time held at Wembley in London but in recent years it has been held at the National Exhibition Centre in Birmingham. Of course, if you live in a big city you are likely to have a better opportunity of visiting such exhibitions. But if your teacher knows of exhibitions, even if they are many miles away, it is always possible for your school to arrange a visit for a party of students. Such an arrangement has the advantage of the teacher being able to give you guidance beforehand, so that you know what to look for.

Look in the advertising columns of your local newspaper or on the notice boards at school or in the local library. Exhibitions are often well advertised.

The best time to visit exhibitions is during your first year of the GCSE course. In the second year you will be coming to the final stages of coursework.

2.13 Yellow Pages

If you are researching into materials, processes, etc., a visit to a *local industry* could prove to be valuable.. They could show you how material is shaped, moulded, coated, assembled, etc., and possibly give you assistance with some production processes involved in your own project. To find such a valuable local source you might look through the *Yellow Pages* Telephone Directory. Companies, businesses, organisations, clubs etc. are all listed under a heading that is appropriate for their speciality. For example, companies concerned with plastics vacuum forming are grouped under the heading of either plastics or vacuum forming. A check in the alphabetical index at the front will tell you whether to look under P or V and will give you the page on which the companies are listed. Under this heading you will find many companies listed in alphabetical order under the company name, e.g. D.V. Components Ltd; London Plastics; etc.

2.14 Audio visual

Television companies, such as Thames, have produced GCSE programmes specially for CDT. These are available on video and perhaps your school has a copy. These can give you general guidance and may suggest ideas to help with your coursework.

Some Examining Groups have also produced *videos*, and these are available for schools to use. All that is necessary is for your teacher to write to the Examining Group and to request a loan of the video tapes, if they are available.

The programme *Tomorrow's World* is often a source of inspiration for topics. Though some of the new developments are often highly sophisticated, some of the products designed for the Third World are quite basic in their use of materials and energy and they do demonstrate how problems can be resolved with limited resources. Such topics are invaluable as a source of ideas.

S O U N D   C A S S E T T E   T A P E S

The Longman GCSE Pass Pack Series has a booklet and a tape which are designed to help you with your coursework as well as your exam. You have a chance of listening to what a Chief Examiner has to say and what he or she is looking for in a piece of coursework. You can also hear students asking the Chief Examiner the sort of questions *you* might ask if you had the opportunity. The advantage of the tape is that you can listen by yourself, with or without headphones, and follow examples and illustrations in the booklet at the same time. You can also replay the tape if you don't understand anything the first time round. These are available in W.H. Smith's and many book shops.

2.15 Universities and polytechnics

Many of these higher educational establishments have a knowledge and expertise in design education. In fact they have departments that are training students to be CDT teachers. You may even have some of their students beginning their teaching experience in your school. If you are fortunate to have the opportunity of meeting a student teacher of CDT you may find that he or she will be willing to help you and may even invite you to their department in the university or polytechnic. You might be able to see the sort of projects they have to do as part of their training.

2.16 Competitions

While you may not be keen to enter a local and/or national design competition, you may find it of value to see the *exhibition* of the entries. This often takes place after the prizes have been awarded. Many CDT candidates find that the work they are doing for their GCSE is appropriate for a competition so that they can 'kill two birds with one stone' by entering part of their coursework for the competition.

In the exhibition of entries you will not only see a product or system that is a solution to a problem but also all the important stages involved, from identifying a need to the evaluation of the solution. In a well-organised exhibition you may pick up some useful hints about presentation. A well-presented exhibition of work can make even a mediocre piece of coursework look impressive. Just put yourself in the position of a visiting assessor and see how *you* would respond to a heap of work, left on a table, compared with work that had been carefully arranged!

The sources for research are almost limitless and though many sources have been outlined in this chapter, there are still other sources that you may find. However, they are most likely to follow from one of the routes we have considered. For example, you may go to an exhibition and meet someone who has similar interests. You can then share your experience and information.

PRESENTING AN ASSIGNMENT

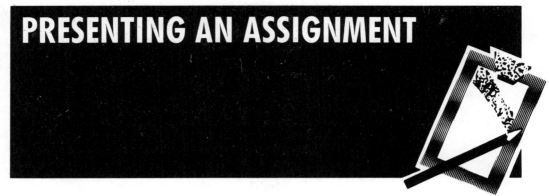

CHAPTER 3

The word 'presentation' has already occurred several times. This topic is so important that we shall deal with it in more detail.

Presentation is all about *communicating*. If you are to communicate your ideas through your work, you must give careful thought to how you *present* your Design Folio and your solution to a problem.

A completed project is represented by a *Folio* and a piece of *practical work* that is related to what has taken place in the Folio. The maximum mark for each part is the same, so you are advised to give both parts equal attention. To put all your energy into the production of a Folio and give very little time and energy to the practical work can lead to drastic results. No matter what your strength happens to be, you must do both parts to the best of your ability.

> **The Design Folio and the practical end product have equal weighting in most syllabuses.**

UNIT 1 PRESENTATION OF THE FOLIO

The Design Folio is a document that stores your complete record of solving a problem from the identification of a need to the evaluation of a solution. The contents should be classified and put in a logical sequence, and it should be organised so that someone else can follow easily what you have entered in your Folio.

The best place to start is to *list* the activities that have to be completed to solve a problem. Then arrange these activities in an appropriate order, explaining how each step was taken towards arriving at the making of a solution. Finally present your evaluation of the solution. Your list may look like this:

> **Aspects to include in your Design Folio.**

a) Identification of a need
b) Research to identify a need
c) Drawing up a Design Brief
d) Analysing the Design Brief
e) Research and investigation resulting from the analysis
f) Developing a variety of ideas
g) Selecting a chosen idea from a number of possibilities
h) Developing a chosen idea in more precise detail
i) Making a Working Drawing
j) Planning a production schedule
k) Making the solution to the problem
l) Evaluating the solution

These are the stages that are looked for in a project. Though the stages might not happen exactly in the same order as given above, it is recommended that yours be very similar.

The stages can become the *title* of each section and the *list of contents* of the Folio. If you use a binder to hold the sheets of paper together, you can put them in order at any time. The plastic Burton Binder is a cheap but efficient method of holding loose sheets of paper together. With a stiff piece of card at the back, and a medium stiff coloured card for the front cover, your work will be kept flat and well protected. (See Fig 1.12 on p. 8.)

Think of your Folio as a book. The cover will have a *title* and the *name of the author*. Inside it will have a *contents list* and it will be divided into *chapters*. Each *page* has a number and this number can be found on the contents list. Since this is a well-established method of presenting information there is good reason for you to adopt a similar approach.

You can still express your individuality, so long as it is clear that you have chosen a method that will readily communicate your project. The use of *audio* and *visual* means may be appropriate for your project and, if this is the case, plan and structure the contents of these so that they follow in a logical sequence. The listener or viewer will then be able readily to understand what you are communicating. Perhaps make use of a jingle to indicate the end of one section and the beginning of the next. Introduce the contents at the beginning and give each section a title. Remember the audiotape or videotape needs to be as carefully structured as a book or Design Folio. You will also have to consider whether your chosen medium enables you to *demonstrate* those skills that are being assessed.

1.1 Identification of a need

A diagram of the type shown in Fig 1.2 (p. 2), but extended more broadly (Fig 2.1, p. 15), is a good way of presenting information clearly and without the use of a lot of words. When you arrive at the 'identification of a need', you should *state your reason* for your decision. Your reason may be apparent to you, but not to a visiting assessor. If there is one thing that an assessor looks for, it is your ability to make *reasoned judgements*. Even if the assessor may not always agree with your reasoning, he or she will give you credit for thinking through your approach to the problem.

1.2 Research

List the areas of research and give precise details of the source. If your information came from a book, state the title and page number. You can also give the name of the author if you think this helps. If your source is a magazine or an article in a journal, you will need to give the date of issue, which is usually clearly printed on the front cover. This is not so that the assessor can check your source of information, but to enable you to refer back to that source, if necessary. However, the assessor is likely to be impressed by your attention to such detail.

> ❝ **Keeping a diary is a useful way of recording information.** ❞

It is often helpful to keep a *diary* or a *small note book* where you store all this type of information, since it is unreasonable to expect you to carry your Folio around with you. Remember that the Southern Examining Group expects you to present your Folio on A2 paper. So, by keeping your notes in a diary, you can enter the important details when you have the facility of a drawing board or table top. You can also give due attention at that point to the quality of printing, layout and style of presentation. If you have a typewriter or wordprocessor you can use this type of equipment to present your information in your Folio.

If, in researching your topic, you wrote letters to companies, organisations, etc., then these, together with the replies, can be pasted on the sheets of the Folio. Take care with the type of paste you use and with the type of paper on which you stick them. You may prefer instead to use a large envelope and to present this, with its contents, as a separate part of the coursework.

1.3 Design Brief

You can use colour, large lettering, etc. to present the Design Brief. Think of it as a main heading which you want to stand out from any other information. Write it on an empty page. This may seem a waste of paper but it will be easier to refer back to when you are *evaluating* possible solutions. It will also make sure that the reader knows what the problem is all about. There is a temptation to use luminous highlighting pens. Although this does help to make information stand out, it can be over used and make the assessor wish for a more 'gentle' approach.

1.4 Analysis

The technique recommended for the presentation of research can also be applied to the analysis, i.e. listing each part as briefly but as concisely as possible. Each part of the analysis can start with a numeral or letter, e.g. (i), (ii), (iii); a), b), c); or 1, 2, 3; etc. This will not only present the details clearly, but will prove helpful when presenting the evaluation later in the Folio. (See sheet 2 of 'Everything in its Place' on p. 83.)

> ❝ **You can present your analysis in the form of a list.** ❞

Again, use can be made of a typewriter or wordprocessor to present such information. It is not recommended that you use letter-press techniques which, though a professional finish can be achieved, are not a sensible use of your valuable time. If you are skilled at using stencils or, better still, have a good quality standard of lettering, then you are recommended to use these types of technique because they are less time consuming.

RESEARCH AND INVESTIGATION RESULTING FROM THE ANALYSIS

The assessor is not looking for a blow-by-blow account of the research carried out. All that is required is a list of people contacted, places visited, equipment (such as construction kits) used, any tests that you may have carried out, questionnaires used, etc. Also make sure to display clearly the results or findings obtained.

Photographic evidence can often play a valuable part in presenting some research, such as the *context* in which a need has been identified. Just a few carefully selected photographs, with a brief word of explanation under each photograph, is all that is needed. Remember that a few *carefully selected* photographs are much better than a large number of photographs which are very similar. It is *quality* and *relevance* that is required, not quantity.

1.5 Developing a variety of ideas

Many pupils are not happy trying to develop ideas through the use of sketches on a large sheet of paper, i.e. A2 or A3. They feel lost and unsure when confronted with two conflicting tasks, one of drawing freely to develop ideas and the other of trying to keep things tidy to reach a high quality of presentation. There are, however, ways of meeting *both* targets. Nevertheless, it should be stressed here that in this part of the Folio it is the *development of ideas* that is by far the most important task; tidying up is much less important.

❝ Try to look at a wide range of possibilities. ❞

The assessor is looking for signs of your ability to develop your ideas, your open-mindedness in looking at a wide range of alternative possibilities, your ability to predict possible advantages or disadvantages, your ability to evaluate one design compared with another, and so on. Nowhere *in this section* is the assessor looking for your ability to draw or to have a feeling for layout and presentation. These qualities can be made apparent in the *development* of a chosen idea.

One way of overcoming this conflict between the development of ideas and good presentation is to do all your sketches, drawing, notes, etc. in a *sketch pad*. Then you can cut out the bits that you think important and relevant and paste them on a sheet of A2 or A3 paper that has a clear heading, such as 'Development of Ideas', 'Initial Ideas', etc. This does not take long to do and is a far better use of your time than redrawing everything just for the sake of presentation.

1.6 Selection of an idea

❝ Give your reasons for selecting a particular idea. ❞

The most important aspect to present here is your *design reasoning*. Much of what you have written in your notes will help you to *select* an idea that is worth developing. The assessor must be able to read your notes, so take care to make sure that your printing is readable. Concise notes are an asset, so there should not be the need for a lot of lengthy writing. For instance, you may have selected a design because it is easy to carry, the materials are readily available, the processes of manufacture are within your capability and the school has the appropriate machines. If so, then just state these reasons in as few words as possible. Perhaps with the reasons as a *list*; e.g.:

1   Easy to carry
2   Materials available
3   Can be made, etc.

1.7 Developing the chosen idea

Here you will need to demonstrate your *ability to draw* and your *understanding of construction*. Good presentation of these skills is important, therefore you will need to concentrate your attention on *communication*. Drawing in three dimensions is commonly used and is a most successful method of communicating the detail of the chosen idea. The drawing can be assembled or exploded. An *assembled* drawing is one that is drawn with all its component parts fitted together. An *exploded* drawing allows you to show more detail because the parts are drawn separated but in such a position that if they were moved towards each other they would fit together. (See Fig 2.2 on pp. 18–19.)

The word *development* in this context means taking the idea on paper and showing how it could be made. It is not necessarily a working drawing, but there is often sufficient detail for you to feel that you could make what is shown. For example, the outline and the thickness of material would suggest that the idea could be made in wood, mainly because the thickness is more appropriate to wood than, say, to metal.

To present such information you can use your artistic skills, and any medium you wish, to give colour and texture and to create the impression that the product actually exists. Architects do this when they give an artistic impression of a building or a new development. The drawing should be large enough for detail to be clearly shown. Though dimensions are not necessary, it is helpful if the *proportions* are about right. You can have a main drawing in the middle of the page, with drawings round the sides giving detail of how one part fits into another or how a gearing and cam mechanism functions. If *ratios* have been considered, these could be calculated and stated on this sheet.

1.8 The working drawing

The method of presenting a working drawing is already clearly defined. For instance, there are correct ways of presenting an Orthographic Projection (see p. 34) and these have been established by the British Standards Institution (BSI). There are many specialised publications, and you should be familiar with the following:

▶ PP 7302   British Standards for Design and Technology in Schools
▶ PP 7307   Graphical Symbols for Use in Schools and Colleges
▶ PP 7308   Engineering Drawing Practice for Schools and Colleges
▶ PP 7310   Anthropometrics: An Introduction for Schools and Colleges
▶ PP 7320   Construction Drawing Practice for Schools

You are not expected to know *all* the detail contained in these publications. They are reference sources for you to use so that you present information using the correct layout, symbol, convention, etc. When an assessor looks at a working drawing that has been represented in Orthographic Projection, he or she will expect to see that you have followed the recommendations laid down by the British Standards Institution. Therefore you are advised to follow the recommendations accurately, just as you would use a dictionary for the spelling of a word.

TYPES OF PENCIL USED FOR DRAFTING

The medium used for presenting an Orthographic Projection drawing is more often than not *pencil*. It is important that you use a sharp pencil because this will give a clean line that is of even density and thickness throughout its length. This may mean that the pencil will require constant sharpening during the course of a single drawing. An H grade pencil needs less sharpening than a B grade pencil and is recommended for this reason. Clutch pencils are more expensive but they are designed to produce much better results.

Just as there are a range of lead grades for the standard pencil, so there are for the lead-holder type of pencil, but in addition there are grades that are suitable for drawing on draughting film. To get good results it is important to use the correct type of pencil on the appropriate material. Polymer-based leads are specially designed for use on draughting films. In draughting, a variety of thickness of lines is recommended, so the leads are available in a *range of diameter thicknesses*. The range includes the following diameters: 0.3mm, 0.5mm, 0.7mm, 0.9mm and 2mm. The 0.3mm and the 0.6mm leads are suitable for the thin construction lines that are used in dimensioning, projection lines, hatching, centre lines, etc. The 0.7mm or 0.9mm leads are suitable for the thicker lines used to show outlines and edges of objects. The important thing to remember is that the difference between a projection line and an outline should be obvious by the difference in the thickness of the line drawn.

BLACK FIBRE-TIPPED PENS

These produce a darker line and give a drawing a more professional look. Unfortunately it is not so easy to remove the line when a mistake has been made. So considerable care and skill is needed when using such a pen.

DRAWING PENS

There are drafting pens that are refillable with a drawing ink that can only be used in drawing pens. Like the pencil leads, they have a range of different diameter-size tips. Not all papers are suitable for ink, so you should test a sample *before* embarking on a drawing. If the ink soaks into the paper and produces what look like little hairs growing from the line, then the paper is definitely *not* suitable. If a clean crisp line is obtained, the ink is remaining on the surface and not soaking into the paper, which means that the paper *is* suitable.

Most tracing papers are suitable and all plastic draughting film is suitable for ink drawings. If you make a mistake on draughting film it is possible to remove the error with a sharp craft

Make sure you present your working drawing correctly.

knife. By gently scratching the ink it will flake off, leaving very little evidence of it having been there at all.

Ink drawings *photocopy* much better than pencil drawings. The detail is very clear and can even be good enough to present in your Folio. Because more care is needed to produce an ink drawing you are advised to draw in pencil on ordinary cartridge paper and then to do the ink drawing by placing a tracing paper or drafting film over the pencil drawing. You can then trace the outlines with an ink drawing pen to produce a very professional finish. (See, for example, Fig 3.1.)

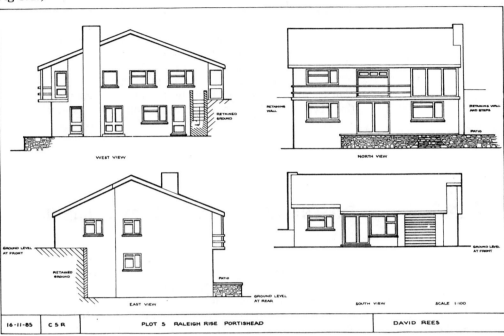

Fig 3.1
Example of drawing in ink

You should *not* colour a working drawing. It is not necessary and, if anything, it might make some detail less clear. This would defeat the purpose of a working drawing.

A working drawing should contain sufficient information for the solution to be made. This means that all the constructional detail should be complete, all the important dimensions given, the materials named, and a cutting and/or parts list correctly presented. (See sheet 4 of Shadow Theatre on p. 74).

An assessor will look for all this information and will look to see if the correct method of presentation has been used. While the assessor will not take off marks for incorrect work, he or she can only award marks for what is correct. So do not throw away your chances of gaining credit when a little care and attention to the standards set by BSI could be of benefit to you.

1.9 Evaluation

This is a very important part of your coursework. While credit is given for the quality of the observations and the judgements that you have made in your evaluation, it is helpful if care has been given to its presentation.

One method of presenting your judgements is to make a list of the details given in your analysis and to just change the *statements* into *questions*. For example, you may have written down in your analysis that:

a) The solution must be portable
b) It must be light
c) It should be attractive, etc.

So in your evaluation you can refer to the same lettering and statements used in the list and write:

	Evaluation	
Criteria	Judgement	Recommendation
a) Is the solution portable?		
b) Is it light?		
c) Is it attractive? etc.		

This type of presentation is easy to follow and it means that each detail that formed part of the analysis can be answered with a *judgement* and followed by a *recommendation* for an improvement.

Assessors prefer an easy-to-follow format, like the one illustrated, rather than a lengthy essay-type answer.

1.10 Planning and presenting a production schedule

Knowing that the solution to the problem has to be made by a certain date it is important for you to *plan a work schedule* that will enable you to meet your deadline. It is also important that you convey that information to the assessor.

Your work plan should be evident in your Design Folio and presented as a part of your coursework. Remember that the Design Folio counts for 50% of the coursework mark and that the coursework, in most cases, counts for as much as 25% of the total marks for the subject.

UNIT 2 PRESENTATION OF PRACTICAL WORK AND/OR THE DESIGN SOLUTION

❝❝ Remember to display the exploratory work that led to the design solution. ❞❞

To arrive at a solution you may have found it necessary to do some *exploratory* practical work, such as making models or mock-ups, testing types of finishes, etc. These should form part of the package you display for assessment. It is important to display such material so that the purpose, the sequence of steps and the findings that have led to the development of a design solution can be clearly seen. It may be appropriate to *label* each practical sample, and to give a *brief comment* explaining its purpose, function, etc. Such evidence can be mounted on card and presented on a vertical display board.

The final design solution may need little extra work to improve its appearance, if all stages of its manufacture have been completed. The main thing you should now be concerned with is *how to exhibit* your work to the best advantage.

UNIT 3 EXHIBITION OF COURSEWORK

The responsibility for presenting the coursework for assessment at the end of the course usually falls upon your teacher. This is mainly because the candidates are not always available to do the task themselves. If you are fortunate enough to be available, and you are able to be involved in exhibiting your work, you can give some care and attention to *presenting* your work to the best advantage. No Examining Group, however, allocates marks for an exhibition in their marking schemes. But good presentation will help to ensure that the assessor sees all that should be seen. If work is poorly displayed, it is possible that some of it will be overlooked.

Fig 3.2 shows how a candidate has exhibited her coursework to the best advantage. Good use has been made of presenting a selection of sheets from the Design Folio on a display board. The sheets have been mounted on a coloured card and care has been taken with the layout of each sheet. The name of the candidate and the topic that had been chosen are clearly shown, together with other information to guide the assessor through the project.

The candidate who produced the piece of work shown in Fig 3.3 has obviously gone to some trouble to make sure that the assessor knows where to look for the different stages, and to show that each of the stages has been covered. The title page of the Design Folio shows clearly all the information that is needed, i.e. the candidate's name and the title of the assignment. The illustration is neatly presented and adds interest and individuality. The practical realisation is placed near the Design Folio and the package is complete.

Fig 3.4 shows the Design Folio and practical work of another candidate. The practical work appears to be unfinished, and placing it on top of the Folio in this way hides the identity of the candidate and the name of the project. The assessor has to move the practical work to one

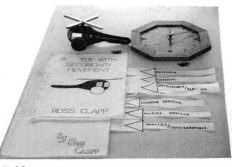

Fig 3.3
Exhibition of coursework

Fig 3.2
Exhibition of coursework

Fig 3.4
Exhibition of coursework

side and attempt to relate the Folio to the bits and pieces. A display of this kind does not convey a good impression and an assessor will already be making some predictions about the quality of the work displayed. From what you can see, *you* will no doubt have formed an impression and it is certain that your impression and the assessor's are going to be similar! Though the true quality of the work is not going to be changed by the display, the candidate has made a poor start. In this example it is unlikely that the work inside the folio will be of a high standard, showing clear evidence of organisation and presentation qualities. However, it is still possible for the *analysis* and the *design work* to be of a high standard. But if the organisation and communication skills are weak, many aspects of design thinking and reasoning will be lost.

So you see, it *is* helpful if the coursework is displayed with care.
You may also have to display work that was done as part of a Design and Realisation paper. This is the case if the Examining Group decides the topics and context of the project and you have to complete the assignment in the time specified.

LEAG set three topics from which you do one during the final term of the course. You can spend as little or as much time as you wish on the *designing*, but you have a minimum of 5 hours in which to complete the *realisation*. In other words, the complexity of the project should mean that you need to spend a minimum of 5 hours making it. If the realisation can be made in less than 5 hours, then it is likely that it is insufficiently demanding for a 16-year-old.

MEG set a theme and candidates have to identify a need that can be accepted within the theme. For example, one year the theme was 'Learning Aids', another year it was 'Games'. So you see that the themes are not very restricting and you can find something that is of interest to you. MEG state that a maximum time of 20 hours of normal school time should be used to complete the project. The candidate can, however, make sensible modifications to the design during its production in order that the solution can be made within the time available. The Examining Group believes that being able to work to a schedule is important and this is why the *maximum* of 20 hours is imposed.

Working on this type of assignment is no different from your ordinary coursework. You have to start with the identification of a need, write a Design Brief and analysis, conduct research, etc., and end with a product evaluation. So the package of a *Design Folio* and a piece of *practical work* will appear to be the same as a coursework assignment. Because it *is* very similar to coursework, further information about the Design and Realisation paper is given below.

> **UNIT 4**   # DESIGN AND REALISATION PAPER

LEAG set three topics from which you select one and complete it during the spring term and the first part of the summer term of your final year. The themes in past years have included 'Energy Conversion Application', and 'Movement in Two Planes'.

4.1 Starting the design assignment

Here we briefly outline the three problems set in 1988. Problem A was about shadow theatre (the projection of a shadow on a screen). This problem could be resolved with skills and understanding involving *mechanisms*, but also provides an opportunity to demonstrate *aesthetic* qualities. A basic understanding of *construction* would also be necessary. The second problem, Problem B, has an *engineering* flavour. It requires an understanding of a mechanism that will produce accurate and reliable movements for a seed sowing device to function efficiently. The aesthetic quality has a low priority, and may even be ignored, in this type of problem. Problem C involved 'a Wall Plaque in relief' and could be resolved without any need to understand mechanisms but it does require an understanding of *colour, shape* and *form*. You also need to know how to use them to depict movement on a static wall plaque. Therefore you could say that this problem has an *artistic* flavour. So you see that these three problems cover a wide range of interests and skills and you should choose a problem that matches your own interests and skills.

4.2 When you have made your choice

Having decided which problem you wish to attempt you need to carry out some research. It is unlikely that you are already familiar with 'shadow theatres', 'seed sowers', etc., so you will need to use the available resources, such as books, magazines, museums, people and firms, to find out some background information. All the information you acquire must be recorded and arranged in a *Research and Investigation Folio*. Though you will not be expected to do much of your design thinking in this Folio, it must be presented with your coursework so that you can be given credit for the background research you have done.

The method of carrying out this research is left entirely to you. The presentation of the Research and Investigation Folio should show *evidence* of your findings, and should be similar in format to a Design Folio. It should have a protective covering front and back; the top cover should have a *title*, e.g. Shadow Theatre or Seed Sower, and include your name. You can, of course, give the cover some individual identity, but be careful not to obscure the title and your name. You might organise the Research and Investigation Folio so that the information you receive from your enquiries is kept together. If need be, you could use a title for each page or pages to show the *origin of your sources*, e.g. 'Museums Visited', 'Observations Made', 'Books Used', 'Firms Contacted', and so on. This sorting out of your research material into *sections* will help you to use your Folio efficiently. It will also help you to complete your Design Answer Sheet, where you have to give a summary of your research and investigation. (See pp 32–4.)

Because the range of research and investigation will vary according to where you live and the type of resources that are available, it is impossible to outline the precise information that should be included in your Research and Investigation Folio. A range of possible sources of information for your project is outlined on pp. 16–24 above.

4.3 Design Answer Sheets

Although the work done on these sheets is marked separately from the course, it none the less has to be completed during your normal school lessons. So in many ways it is just another piece of work done during the course. That is why it is appropriate to include a section dealing with the presentation on the Design Answer Sheets in a book that is concerned with coursework. In any case, whatever syllabus you are studying, the following outline will put into practice many of the points relevant to all syllabuses.

The Design Answer Sheets for LEAG consist of just four sheets of good quality A3 paper that have been designed to take you through a number of stages. Other Examining Groups that include this component in their exam use a similar format.

Section 1a): State the problem chosen

The first section, 1a), asks you to state the problem chosen. You can just state A, B, C or 1, 2, 3, but it is perhaps better to give the brief title that was given on the paper, i.e. 'Shadow Theatre', 'Seed Sowing Device', or 'Wall Plaque in Relief'. Then you should go one stage further by saying 'Shadow Theatre for 5–7-year-old Children'; or 'Seed Sowing Device for Peas'; or 'Wall Plaque for a Food Transport Company'. In other words, try to be more *specific* than the theme which is given.

Section 1b): Summary of your Folio (Research and Investigation)

In the small space available, you list a summary of the work you did in *preparation* for solving your chosen problem. This would include details such as title of books used, with the page or pages which provided you with research information; and the names of museums, exhibitions, etc. that you contacted or visited. State briefly what use you made of construction kits, mock- ups or models to establish practical information. List the observations you made and the questionnaires you used. Remember that you are asked only for a *summary* rather than for a detailed account of how you arranged to meet your friend at 10 a.m. to go to a museum and that you took your sketch pad, etc. Only factual information directly related to the research is needed here. Short statements of facts, presented in a list, is what is required in this section (and in similar sections for other Examining Groups).

Section 1c): Analysis of the problem

You are asked specifically to 'list' the important points that you will consider in preparing your design. If you have chosen the shadow theatre problem, your list could include any of the following:

a) Where the theatre is to be used
b) The capabilities of young children to operate a theatre
c) The number of young children that are going to view the theatre
d) The type of story, nursery rhyme or tale that is suitable for young children
e) A safe light source for making the shadows
f) Materials suitable for a shadow theatre
g) Storing the theatre when not in use
h) The need for the theatre to be portable
i) The most suitable height for viewing and operating the theatre
j) The design of the two animated characters you intend to use so that they will be easily recognised
k) The method by which each character is made to move
l) The appearance of the theatre.

> **Analysis for designing a Shadow Theatre for five- to seven-year-old children.**

Such an analysis *list* is what the assessor is looking for. Factors such as the availability of materials, suitable manufacturing equipment, the time available, and personal experience and expertise are important considerations but these apply to *any* problem. They do not gain so much credit at this stage as those points that relate specifically to the problem. So make sure you put down the specific detail first, then if you have room, you can add the more general detail.

Section 2: My first ideas and decisions

Some of the ideas you made a note of in your Research and Investigation Folio may be selected and presented in this section. You can also go further with any new ideas that are now developing in your mind. Use *annotated sketches* so that you tell the assessor *why* you think a particular idea is feasible or not. You are asked (by LEAG) to put a tick against those ideas you are going to use: so when you do this, just state briefly *why* you have chosen that particular idea. Be as *specific* as you possibly can with your answer, because such comments as 'I like it' say very little and therefore earn little credit. Try to relate your comments to the points you listed in the *analysis*, e.g. 'this idea is easy for young children to operate', or 'I like the outline of the characters because they are easily recognised', and so on. You are also asked by LEAG to add details of materials to be used. So name *specific materials*, such as mild steel, acrylic, parana pine, etc.

Section 3: Proposed design

This sheet is available for you to present your proposed design in detail. Though it is *not* intended that you present a working drawing here, it is intended that you present *sufficient detail* for anyone to see how all the parts of your design fit together. You may use whatever *type* of drawing is appropriate, and of course it is probably advisable to select a type that you can do well. Normally you would be expected to present your proposed design in a three-dimensional drawing or drawings. This is also an opportunity for you to demonstrate your drawing ability.

An *Isometric Grid* is provided by LEAG for candidates who prefer using a grid when drawing in three dimensions. However, there is also blank space for you to choose whichever method of presentation you wish to use, e.g. two dimensional, single-point perspective, two-point perspective, assembled or exploded views (see p. 18).

Whichever method you use to present your proposed idea, it must be clear, well proportioned and fully detailed. This means that the material thickness must be appropriate to the material chosen, e.g. a piece of wood should normally be thicker than a piece of plastic or metal, given that the lengths and widths of each piece of material are similar.

Section 4: Working drawing

Here there is space for presenting the *working drawing*. Though you have possibly given a lot of detail in Section 3, and you could possibly make what you have designed from those details, the working drawing goes at least one stage further. A working drawing must be drawn *to scale*. It should be either the same size as the solution when it is made, or it should be proportionally smaller or larger. More often than not, the working drawing is either the same size or smaller than the finished product. There are recommended scales which you are advised to use. These can be found in *British Standards Publications PP 7308*, p. 2.

The most commonly used method of presenting a working drawing is in *Orthographic Projection*. This type of projection is two dimensional and has the advantage that all surfaces can be drawn as true lengths and shapes in at least one view. Therefore, if your drawing is the same size as the product to be made, you can put your piece of material on the drawing to check that your marking out, cutting length, etc., agree with the details given in your drawing.

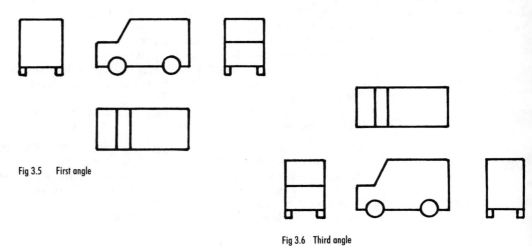

Fig 3.5   First angle

Fig 3.6   Third angle

There are two types of Orthographic Projection, *First Angle* (see Fig 3.5) and *Third Angle* (see Fig 3.6). You can use either, but not both, on the same drawing.

The examples should help you see the differences. It is a question of knowing *where* to place the views. So if you do have difficulty, perhaps you can remember that in *First Angle* the views are 'opposite' sides, i.e. what you see from the left side you draw on the right side, what you see from the right side you draw on the left side, and what you see from above you draw underneath. By way of contrast, *Third Angle* is the 'same' sides, i.e. what you see from the left you draw on the left, what you see from the right you draw on the right, and what you see from above you draw above.

The views should be *dimensioned* and presented using the standards recommended in British Standards PP 7308.

Finally you should complete a *cutting list* of the materials to be used. The *length, width*, and *thickness* of each piece of material should be given. If you require to use other accessories, such as nails, screws, nuts, rivets, etc., you should give the *sizes* and the *quantity*. If you require adhesives, solders, etc., you should give the *specific name* or type.

When the Design and Realisation paper is completed, which should be no later than the date given on the front sheet, the sheets must be fastened together and given to your teacher. He or she will then send them to the examiner who will be marking your work.

You should check that your name, centre number and your candidate number are on each of the sheets submitted and that all the sheets are fastened together in the correct order and the correct way round. Even if you did not use all the sheets, you are advised to send all of them in. Otherwise the examiner may see that a sheet is missing and assume that it is still at your school with some work on it, and so check with the school to see if they can send the missing sheet or sheets. This would not please the examiner and would certainly not form a good impression.

4.4 Making your solution

Before you start to 'mark out' your material, you should carefully consider how you are going to use your time for the making to the best advantage. This requires you to write out a *planning schedule*. There are marks available for planning and, while your teacher can see how well you organise your time in the workshop, it is helpful for you to put down on paper what you plan to do each lesson. Writing a plan down will also have the advantage of making you *think* about each stage, the *order* in which each stage should be taken, and *how long* to allow for each stage so that the product is completed on time. You can put the planning schedule in your Research and Investigation Folio.

If we assume that you have six school weeks in which to make and complete your solution, your basic plan could look like that in the example below.

Week	Date	Work to be done	Work done
6	3 March	Marking out and cutting to length	
5	10 March	Shaping and bending	
4	17 March	Vacuum forming, trimming and drilling	
3	24 March	Joining parts together	
	Holiday Break		
2	14 April	Cleaning up and checking function	
1	21 April	Spraying, polishing	

If you completed the making by this last date on your schedule, it would give you time to complete the final stage, which is to *test* your solution and to write an *evaluation*.

By breaking the making into stages, you can see if you are on target for completing your work. On the other hand, you can also see if you are getting behind and need to speed up your rate of progress.

You could take your planning a stage further by working out what you need to complete in *each lesson*. You may have two or three lessons each week, and so you might plan what you hope to do in lesson 1, lesson 2, and lesson 3 of each week.

Your planning schedule could then be more detailed and look something like this:

Week	Lesson	Work to be done	Work done
	1	Mark out all parts. Check with working drawing	
6	2	Complete marking out and checking. Cut parts to size	
	3	Clean up cut edges and check on working drawing	
	1	Make former for bending part A	
5	2	Smooth surfaces that come in contact with part A	
	3	Prepare material for bending. Check that vacuum forming machine is available for use next lesson	
	1	Vacuum form part B and trim edges	
4	2	Drill holes and file, scrape and polish edges	
	3	Check and make sure all parts fit accurately	
	1	Prepare cramps and jigs	
3	2	Bond parts A and B together	
	3	Clean up part AB and bond part C with part AB	
		Holiday Break	
	1	Remove excess glue and cement	
2	2	Clean joins and polish	
	3	Check function and adjust where necessary	
	1	Prepare for spraying, mask work, and spray	
1	2	Polish parts A and C	
	3	Final check on function and finish	

The above planning schedule is a guide to the progress being made. There will be times when you get ahead of your estimated schedule, and there will be times when you get behind in your estimated schedule. So do accept that the schedule is only a guide to help you get all your work done on time.

4.5 Evaluation

The *final appraisal* of your solution is important. You now judge its value against the problem and the needs you have identified. So if you attempted the shadow theatre problem, and you designed it for children between the ages of 5 and 7 years, then you could make your first judgement by seeing how well that age group of children responded to your theatre. You should find it quite easy to see if the children watched with interest, laughed, clapped, wanted to be involved, etc. Or, at the other extreme, you should be able to see if the children were lacking in interest by not watching, by talking amongst themselves and by looking round for something else to do. *You* have to judge how well your design fulfilled the needs of these children. An *observation* of their response would be a good way of starting your evaluation. Then you could use the statements in your analysis of the problem and assess how well these were achieved. For example (taken from the analysis on p. 33):

a) Did the theatre suit the place where it was to be used?
b) Were the children able to operate the theatre?
c) Did the theatre suit the number of children watching?
d) Was the story, nursery rhyme, suitable?
e) Was the light source safe?
f) Were the materials suitable?

You should answer each of these questions as objectively as you can, and in as few words as possible. Here are a few answers that could apply to the questions given above.

a) Yes, the theatre was designed to stand on a table and two children were able to sit behind the theatre comfortably.
b) With some difficulty. The children had difficulty keeping the characters the correct distance from the screen in order to give a sharp shadow.
c) The largest group could be no more than ten children.
d) Yes, they liked the spider coming down by Miss Muffet.
e) Yes, two large battery torches were used.
f) No. The screen was made of paper and this got torn.

Having answered the questions as honestly and as objectively as you can, you should now make *recommendations* that would improve the theatre, or suggest alternative ways of making it so that it could be made more easily. You would only make these recommendations where you *identified weaknesses*. So, from the example given above, your response to b) and f) would provide the opportunity for recommendations.
For instance:

b) Guides should be fitted to keep the characters a suitable distance from the screen.
f) A tougher material, such as white linen, should be used for the screen.

An evaluation giving this depth of detail is bound to gain a lot of credit. You could also present your evaluation as a *chart* so that it is easy to follow, perhaps using these three headings:

Criteria	Observation	Recommendation
a) Did the theatre suit the place where it is to be used?	Yes. The theatre stood on a table and two children were able to move the characters.	None

The *criteria* by which you assess the value of a product is the *analysis* turned into *questions*. So your a), b), c), d), etc. listed on p. 36 go in the first column. The *observations* you made in judging how well your solution worked go in the next column, and the *recommendations for improvement* go in the third column. To allow enough room for this, you will need to turn your chart round so that the writing runs parallel to the long edge of the sheet of paper.

The completed evaluation can be presented in your Research and Investigation Folio where it will be assessed as part of your coursework.

Summary

Your coursework-type package for the Design and Realisation paper should include two main parts, a Folio and a Practical Solution.

Your Folio should contain the following:

▶ cover with title and your name
▶ design brief
▶ analysis
▶ research and investigation
▶ development of ideas
▶ selected idea for detailing
▶ a detailed idea
▶ working drawing
▶ cutting list
▶ evaluation.

Your Practical Solution should be completed so that you have demonstrated the following abilities:

▶ to plan, organise your time and resources so that you can complete the making of your solution
▶ to use the appropriate techniques and materials
▶ to work accurately
▶ to produce a quality of finish
▶ to use safe working methods

See Chapter 4, pp. 68–76, for an example of a student's response to the shadow theatre problem.

UNIT 5 MARK SCHEMES

A mark scheme is a detailed account of what you have to do to get the marks that have been allocated. You will have seen in Chapter 1, pp. 10–14, some examples of *mark allocation*. The mark allocation tells you just how many marks are available for each section. The mark scheme goes one stage further by telling you what you have to do to get a specific number of marks in each section, and just how many marks you will get if you have only done parts of the section. Remember, you will gain marks for what you have done; marks are not taken away for what you have not done. So the more you do and complete, the better your chances are of getting the mark that you deserve.

The coursework mark scheme is in two parts. One part is used to assess your *designing ability* and the other is used to assess your *making ability*.

5.1 Assessing your designing ability

Your Design Folio should provide all the evidence that is necessary to show how well you perform as a designer. Here then is a mark scheme used by SEG to assess your designing ability. The principles involved are generally applicable to the other Examining Groups.

SEG MARK SCHEME

The assessment of coursework: Design Folios
---

a) Identification of problem   marks

Band 7   Can react at a low level to suggestions but shows little   1
               understanding of the purpose of a design brief.

Band 6	Can react at a low level to suggestions but unable to create a brief which identifies a suitable design objective without considerable assistance.	2
Band 5	Can respond at a low level to suggestions and prepare a brief but may not recognise that it will limit the potential of the finished project.	3
Band 4	Able to identify a problem only with assistance but then capable of constructing a brief with a reasonable design objective.	4–6
Band 3	Can independently identify a problem and with assistance produce a design brief that outlines the design objective.	7–8
Band 2	Can independently identify a problem and produce a suitable brief with a clear design objective.	9
Band 1	Can independently identify an original problem area and produce a brief which clearly outlines the design objectives.	10

b) Analysis of problem, investigation, initial ideas   marks

Band 7	A shallow analysis which identifies only the most obvious design criteria. A severely limited investigation of the problem area. Initial ideas that are based on one approach/principle.	1–2
Band 6	An analysis that identifies simple design requirements. Some investigation using obvious sources. Initial ideas that are variations of one approach/principle, and lacking originality.	3–5
Band 5	An analysis that identifies design requirements of a less important nature. A limited number of elements in the problem area investigated; with some obvious omissions. Initial ideas show little variety of approach/principle.	6–8
Band 4	An adequate analysis. A sound investigation but fails to identify a number of crucial design requirements. An adequate range of ideas with some variety of approach/principle, but with little originality.	9–11
Band 3	An analysis that identifies a number of important design requirements. A detailed investigation of the problem area. An adequate range of ideas, some of which are imaginatively conceived.	12–14
Band 2	An analysis that identifies most of the major design requirements. A thorough investigation of the problem area using several sources. A varied range of imaginative initial ideas.	15–17
Band 1	A complete and detailed analysis. A thorough first-hand investigation of the problem area using a wide variety of sources. A wide range of imaginative initial ideas.	18–20

c) Development of chosen idea   marks

Band 7	Only minor amendments to an initial idea, with little or no information given about materials and construction.	1–2
Band 6	Some elementary developments of an idea in relation to two of the following four elements: function; appearance; materials; and construction.	3–5
Band 5	Some development of the chosen idea/approach in relation to three of the following four elements: function; appearance; materials; and construction.	6–8

Band 4	Some development of the chosen idea/approach in relation to three of the following four elements: function; appearance; materials; and construction.	9–11
Band 3	The chosen idea or approach is developed with at least one imaginative detail. An ability to make judgements in relation to three of the following four elements: function; appearance; materials; and construction.	12–14
Band 2	Good development of the chosen idea/approach with some imaginative detail. An ability to make sound judgements in relation to all of the following: function; appearance; materials; and construction.	15–17
Band 1	A comprehensive and imaginative development of the chosen idea or approach. An ability to make sound judgements in relation to all of the following: function; appearance; materials; and construction.	18–20

d) Quality of graphical communication which includes a production drawing

marks

Band 7	A low level of graphic skill using only basic techniques executed in a manner which severely limits the development of design ideas and fails to provide useful information that would enable manufacture to proceed.	1–2
Band 6	An ability to communicate ideas at a very simple level using the most basic techniques which limit the development of design ideas and provide insufficient information to allow manufacture to proceed effectively.	3–5
Band 5	A basic level of graphic skills that enables design ideas and the information necessary for manufacture to be communicated at a low level.	6–8
Band 4	A level of graphic skills that conveys ideas at an adequate level, but does not provide enough detail to enable the manufacturing process to proceed smoothly.	9–11
Band 3	A sound level of graphic skills that adequately illustrates design ideas and provides enough information for manufacture to proceed.	12–14
Band 2	Good graphic techniques that convey ideas clearly and provide sufficient information to enable the manufacturing process to proceed effectively.	15–17
Band 1	A very high level of graphic communication using a wide range of appropriate methods and techniques to illustrate design ideas and to develop the manufacturing process.	18–20

e) Evaluation

marks

Band 7	An evaluation that is largely descriptive and shows little evidence of awareness of the deficiencies of an unfinished product.	1
Band 6	One or two simple criteria used to compare the solution with the original design brief on completion of the project.	2
Band 5	A number of factors commented on, on completion of the project, but many significant factors omitted.	3

Band 4	Many design criteria identified in the analysis of the problem commented on both during and on completion of the project, but with some significant factors not considered in both cases.	4–6
Band 3	An evaluation that contains much judgement with some minor factors omitted at the end of the project, but lacking in critical comments during the design stage.	7–8
Band 2	An evaluation which contains considerable critical judgement both during and at the end of the project, with only minor factors omitted. Some evidence of testing to arrive at judgements.	9
Band 1	A comprehensive and critical evaluation of the project at all stages of its development with design modifications, as a result of relevant testing, suggested.	10

The assessment of coursework: Design Folios

This is the mark scheme used by teachers who are preparing candidates for the Southern Examining Group's CDT, Design and Realisation. You will see from mark schemes used by other Examining Groups that they are all very similar. The mark scheme is used in the first place to help your *teacher* arrive at a fair mark for all candidates. But looking at such a scheme will help *you* know what you have to do to gain credit.

Though you will have written a suitable Design Brief in your Design Folio, you and your teacher will know just how much assistance was necessary for a Design Brief to be written. The more you depended upon the teacher, the less contribution *you* made. So the teacher has to decide which of the seven bands describes you best of all. *You* could also see which description describes you best of all; it is hoped that you and your teacher would arrive at the same conclusion.

Having decided which of the seven bands describe you best of all, it has to be decided whereabouts you fit within the band if a range of marks is allocated to a band. Are you in the middle, or are you at the top or bottom end? If you are in the middle, it means that the description is a fairly accurate summary of your performance. It is when a decision has to be made at either end of the band that it can become a little more difficult. This is because the next band may also have to be considered. Let, us suppose a decision has to be made between the top of band 4 and the bottom of band 3. In other words, is your response worth 6 out of 10 or 7 out of 10? The most likely deciding factor in this situation is just *how much assistance* from the teacher was necessary. The more independence you have been able to display, the more likely you are to get 7 out of 10.

Getting started is one of the most difficult parts of designing, which is why so much importance is placed upon *independence*. Some candidates need so much help that they require the Design Brief to be written for them before they can get started. So it is only fair to award the higher marks to those who made the effort and were able to come up with a suitable Design Brief themselves.

WJEC has a very similar scheme. However, here it should be mentioned that the Examining Group sets five topics from which the candidate can choose one, and if the candidate prefers to do one of his or her own then there is an opportunity for this to happen. So now let us compare the two systems. The allocation of 10 marks for the first part to be assessed is identical but the requirements are different. As you read through the Assessment of the Design Brief below, you will see that an analysis and an identification of likely problems are required.

A statement of the Brief

An analysis of the Brief to identify and specify the design requirements.
An identification of likely problems involved.
An identification of further information likely to be needed.

> (At this stage it may be possible for candidates to write a precise and detailed design specification. However, it may be necessary to carry out further investigations before this is possible.)

Then to see how the 10 marks are divided an assessment grid is used (see p. 41). The assessment grid is designed to be used for sections with different mark weightings so that when the marks are out of 5, the first column is used. When the

Work to be considered . . .		Maximum marks		
		5	10	20
excellent in every respect		5	9–10	17–20
of a good standard		4	7–8	13–16
satisfactory/average grade	Award a mark within this range	3	5–6	9–12
rather poor/weak		2	3–4	5–8
very poor/weak		1	1–2	1–4
unacceptable/unsuitable		0	0	0

section being marked is out of 10, the second column is used. For sections marked out of 20, the third column is used.

The Midland Examining Group (MEG) has a similar approach to the Southern Examining Group (SEG) in that *descriptions* are given of what is expected to be achieved in order to get certain levels of marks. As a further guide to what the range of marks mean, three classifications have been made: *low achievement*, *medium achievement* and *high achievement*. The MEG mark scheme below shows this and indicates how these three classifications are further subdivided.

MEG MARK SCHEME

1   Problem identification, analysis and investigation (15 marks)   marks

   a)   Low achievement (0–4 marks)

      i)   No statement of the problem, little or no investigation or analysis.   0–2

      ii) Problem vaguely stated, scope of investigation and analysis very   3–4
           limited.

   b)   Medium achievement (5–10 marks)

      i)   Problem identified, superficial investigation and analysis of some   5–7
           of the factors involved leading to imprecise design specification.

      ii) Problem identified, investigation and analysis of most of the   8–10
           important factors involved, including constraints, leading to
           reasonably clear specification.

   c)   High achievement (11–15 marks)

      i)   Clearly identified problem, investigation and analysis of all the   11–13
           important factors involved leading to a clear specification.

      ii) Clearly identified problem, investigation and analysis of all the   14–15
           factors involved leading to complete design specification.

2   Generation and development of ideas (25 marks)

   a)   Low achievement (0–7 marks)

      i)   One solution suggested, little or no evidence of development of   0–3
           ideas.

      ii) One solution proposed, some evidence of the development of   4–7
           limited ideas.

   b)   Medium achievement (8–15 marks)

      i)   More than one solution proposed, one of which is chosen and   8–11
           developed slightly to meet some of the requirements of the
           specification.

      ii) Several solutions proposed, one of which is developed to meet   12–15
           the major requirements of the specification.

   c)   High achievement (16–25 marks)

      i)   Various ideas which are different in kind, principle or approach   16–20
           are proposed, considered and developed to meet most of the
           requirements of the specification.

ii) Various different solutions each of which differ in kind, principle or approach are proposed and considered, one of which is then developed to reach an optimum solution which meets the requirements of the design specification.   21–25

3   Realisation of design solutions (46 marks)

a)   Low achievement (0–14 marks)

i)   The solution will exhibit a low level of craftsmanship and will not be successfully completed. There will be little or no attempt to make sensible modifications where required. Very little or no planning will have been carried out.   0–5

ii)   The solution will exhibit a low level of craftsmanship, will be mainly complete, and will satisfy the specifications with a limited degree of success. Some attempts will have been made to modify the design solution where required. Planning will be restricted to the immediate task and will rely on prompting.   6–14

b)   Medium achievement (15–31 marks)

i)   The solution will exhibit a reasonable level of craftsmanship, will be largely complete and will function as intended. Some modifications will have been incorporated. Most of the realisation will be planned in advance.   15–23

ii)   The solution will exhibit a good level of craftsmanship, will be complete and will function as intended. Sensible modifications to improve the design will have been incorporated. Most of the realisation will be planned in advance.   24–31

c)   High achievement (32–46 marks)

i)   Solutions will exhibit a high standard of craftsmanship, will be complete and will meet most of the requirements of the design specification. The design will have been improved and developed where required. The realisation will have been planned to specify an effective order for the sequence of operations.   32–40

ii)   Solutions will be completed to an exceptional standard of craftsmanship and will meet the requirements of the design specification. The design will have been developed and improved where required. The realisation will have been thoroughly planned to specify an effective order for the sequence of operations.   41–46

Safety (4 marks)

Limited understanding of safe working procedures and required reminding of safe workshop practice.   0–2

Good understanding of safe working procedures and worked safely with the normal level of supervision.   3–4

Though the word 'independent' does not appear in this mark scheme, the teachers who do the first assessment of the coursework take account of how independently a candidate has worked.

The other Examining Groups adopt similar procedures to those already illustrated and to outline the mark scheme of each Examining Group would only be repeating what has already been covered in this part of the assessment.

5.2 What an examiner is looking for

What the examiners are looking for is usefully described in the London and East
Anglian Group's table, shown below.

	Design	Planning	Making	Evaluation
Outstanding	Understands and analyses a brief. Generates a wide range of proposals. Makes well-reasoned decisions. Produces clear and comprehensive drawings.	Prepares a logical and realistic plan, correctly detailing materials, tools and operations needed to produce an artefact to a defined standard and within all relevant constraints.	Uses tools safely and correctly, with skill and sensitivity. Works confidently and accurately, produces a good finish. Adapts to changing circumstances.	Carries out a full and critical appraisal of the product. Accurately identifies and describes its strengths and weaknesses. Offers proposals for its improvement.
Average	Identifies the essential features of a design task. Settles on a solution, often based on a known form. Produces understandable sketches covering major details.	Plans the major stages of a scheme, which usually needs modification to match available tools, materials, costs and time.	With some supervising produces work within specific requirements. The quality of the work is usually adequate but quality may be sacrificed to achieve completeness.	Compares product with design brief. Shows awareness of functions, aesthetics and cost but rarely makes detached and unbiased judgements.
Weak	Depends on questions and suggestions from the teacher to generate at least one solution to a design problem although response may not always be appropriate. Reproduces conventional ideas. Drawings produced need explanations.	Can list the steps required to execute a familiar task. Able to detail individual steps within a longer term plan produced by the teacher.	Given supervision, assistance, time and encouragement, can follow an instruction sheet and produce an acceptable end product, although not always at the first attempt.	Has difficulty in accepting the need for an evaluation stage. Has a disproportionate concern with functional aspects in terms of success and failure.

We will now look in more detail at what is expected for 'outstanding' in Design,
Planning and Evaluation, which together form your *Design Folio*. Also included in this
table is what is expected of a candidate in the *making*, which we will deal with in
more detail later in this chapter.

D E S I G N

'Understands and analyses a design brief'

This means that the examiner is looking to see how well you can *identify a need* and
can understand the situation in order to be able to write a *Design Brief*. You must
then follow this chapter with an *analysis*, an example of which you can find on page 33
of this chapter.

'Generates a wide range of proposals'

In order to 'generate a wide range of proposals', it is necessary to do some *research*,
and details of how to obtain information is well covered in Chapter 2, pp. 16–24. So
the examiner is looking to see *evidence* of this, such as drawings, notes, pictures,
details of visits, results of questionnaires, etc., in your Folio. The next detail the
examiner will look for is how broad your thinking is when developing ideas. The wider
the range of possibilities considered, the better your chances of doing well in this
section. Keep an open mind and look at all sorts of possibilities, no matter how
ridiculous the idea may seem at first. Remember, 'a wide range of different ideas' is
the key here.

'Makes well-reasoned decisions'

The only way an examiner can tell if you are making any decisions at all is by reading
the *notes* you put near your sketches. So here the key is to put down your thoughts
and reasons *why* you think one idea is better than another, or the good points and the
weak points about an idea. Even if the examiner does not always agree with your
comments, at least you will gain considerable credit for showing that you have made
reasoned judgements.

'Produces clear and comprehensive drawings'

If the examiner is to *understand* what you have drawn, then your drawings must be
sufficiently clear and sufficiently well detailed. Remember that the examiner should not

have to make any guesses as to what a drawing represents. Sometimes the use of too much shading and colouring may cause you to *lose detail*, and when this happens it means that your communication through drawing is not clear.

PLANNING

Your teacher is the person who will know how well you are organised. A well-organised student is one who knows what has to be done in a lesson *before* entering the room. For example, if you are going into a lesson knowing that you are going to vacuum form a dome, you should already have checked that the material you require is available, that the vacuum forming machine is functioning and will be available for use, and that the tools required for trimming and finishing the edges are all available and in good order. This is regarded as *standard* planning.

The very well-prepared student would do all this and *in addition* would have planned alternative work so that if, for any reason, the work planned could *not* be carried out, no valuable workshop time would be wasted. This is called 'back-up planning'. Your teacher will recognise this and be able to give you credit, but a visiting assessor will not have seen you. So the only way in which you can show evidence of this is to *write out* a simple plan and to put this in your Design Folio. Some planning guidance has been given on pp. 4, 30 and 35. You might also include in the planning schedule a column for materials required, tools required, operations to be performed, etc. The method of planning is usually left entirely to the student. However, the important thing is that there should be some *evidence* of planning in your Folio.

MAKING

Your teacher will be the best judge of how capable you are at making your solution. The visiting assessor will be able to see the end product and will be able to assess things such as accuracy and quality of finish. But what the visiting assessor will *not* know is how safely and correctly you used tools, equipment and machinery. So, many of these qualities will be assessed by your *teacher* and the visiting assessor will accept your teacher's decisions.

When a visiting assessor is looking at a piece of coursework, he or she is using all his or her experience of working with materials to judge how well you have performed. The assessor is likely to look at the product carefully, then pick it up and look underneath and inside, feeling the surfaces and the edges. He or she will then begin forming an impression about the quality of the product. If the product has to perform a *particular function*, then the assessor will *test* it to see how well it works. Having done this,' the assessor will then check the details of the *working drawing* to see how well the product *agrees with* the details given in your drawing. For example, do the dimensions on the product agree with those on the drawing? Are the shape and material stated in the working drawing the same as those in the product? This is checking your ability to work *accurately*. If the assessor sees a noticeable difference between the working drawing and the product, he or she will look at your evaluation to see if there is an *explanation*. Having done all this, the assessor is now in a good position to be able to decide about your ability to make.

To summarise then, the assessor is looking for the following:

▶ good clean finish to all surfaces and edges
▶ constructional and dimensional detail agreeing with the working drawing
▶ how well the product performs.

EVALUATION

The assessor is looking to see how well *you* can identify the weaknesses and strengths in the design of your product. Also, where you do identify weaknesses, what *recommendations* you can make to overcome those weaknesses. This could mean that you would recommend a *different material* and/or a *different process* or method of construction. When making recommendations for change, it is important that they are improvements, and that you can give reasons for your recommendations.

The assessor will look to see how well the evaluation relates to the details given in your Design Brief, analysis and specifications. An example of how to present an evaluation is given on pp. 29 and 36.

CASE STUDY: STUDENT'S RESEARCH AND INVESTIGATION FOLIO

HOW BROADLY WAS THE TOPIC RESEARCHED?

This is the first question your teacher and the visiting assessor are going to ask when looking at the Folio. On sheet 1 the student has outlined three important areas. The first relates to the age group of the children. If we look inside the Folio on sheets 4, 5, and 6 we can see that there is evidence of research concerning children aged 1–2 years, 2–3 years, and 3–5 years. So far so good. The sheets are clearly labelled and easy to follow. What the student says about *each age group* is what the assessor is going to want to know. On sheet 4 the comment is brief and to the point and is a reasonable explanation of what a child between the ages of 1 and 2 years might be expected to do. The same applies to the comments made about the 2–3-year-old and the 3–5-year-old. What would be helpful to the assessor is to know *how* this information was obtained – was it obtained from a book or books, was it obtained by parents responding to a questionnaire, or was it obtained by observation?

Assessor's comment

A brief comment here stating the *source* of the information would help to gain more credit. Obviously the work had been done and it would have taken very little time and effort to write this into the Folio.

The drawings are clear and well presented. The notes are brief and easy to read and describe how the toys help to encourage the child from 1 to 2 to walk, the child from 2 to 3 to co-ordinate its movements, and the child from 3 to 5 to develop its imagination. This is all excellent! It is not however clear, but it could be assumed, that these are examples of toys and that the comments are the student's *own thoughts*. The evidence in the Folio would suggest that the topic had been widely researched.

I HAVE DECIDED TO RESEARCH INTO THE FOLLOWING

MOTOR POWERED TOYS FOR CHILDREN

TO DO THIS I WILL NEED TO INVESTIGATE

1. VARIOUS TOYS FOR DIFFERENT AGE GROUPS
FOR EXAMPLE A TOY THAT JUST RUNS ALONG THE FLOOR COULD BE FOR A YOUNG CHILD THAT IS JUST LEARNING TO CRAWL OR WALK. HOPEFULLY THEY WOULD BE ENCOURAGED TO FOLLOW THE TOY SO IT WOULD PLAY A MAJOR PART IN THE PHYSICAL DEVELOPMENT OF THE CHILD

SAFETY
THIS IS A VERY IMPORTANT FACTOR WHEN DESIGNING A TOY AS CHILDREN HAVE A TENDENCY TO THROW THEIR TOYS AROUND AND PUT THEM IN THEIR MOUTH. SO THE MOTOR AND BATTERIES SHOULD BE CONTAIND SAFELY IN THE TOY AND SUITABLE MATERIALS THAT ARE NOT HARMFUL SHOULD BE USED

MECHANISMS
THE DIFFERENT TYPES OF MECHANISMS FOR EXAMPLE BEVEL GEARS, PULLEYS ETC. WILL NEED TO BE LOOKED AT AND THE VARIOUS WAYS IN WHICH THEY CAN BE USED.

| MOTOR POWERED TOYS FOR CHILDREN | INTRODUCTION TO DESIGN FOLIO | | SHEET Nº 1 |

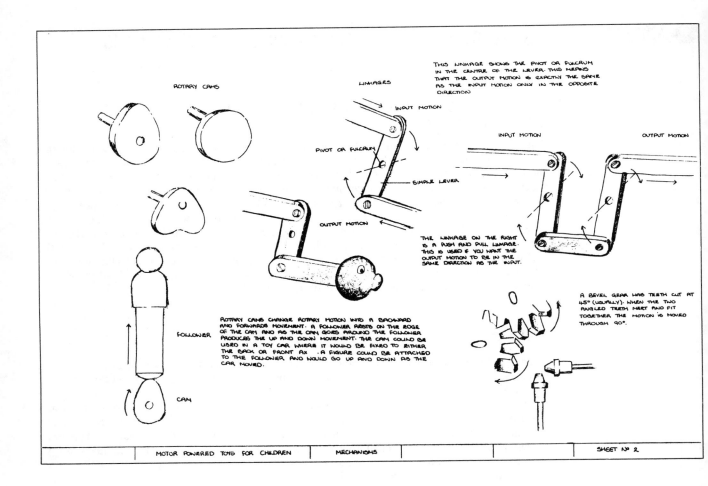

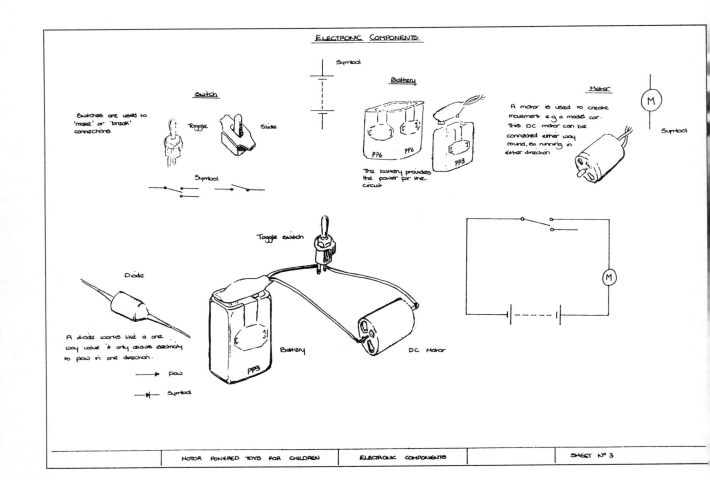

TOYS   FOR   CHILDREN   AGED   1 TO 2 YEARS

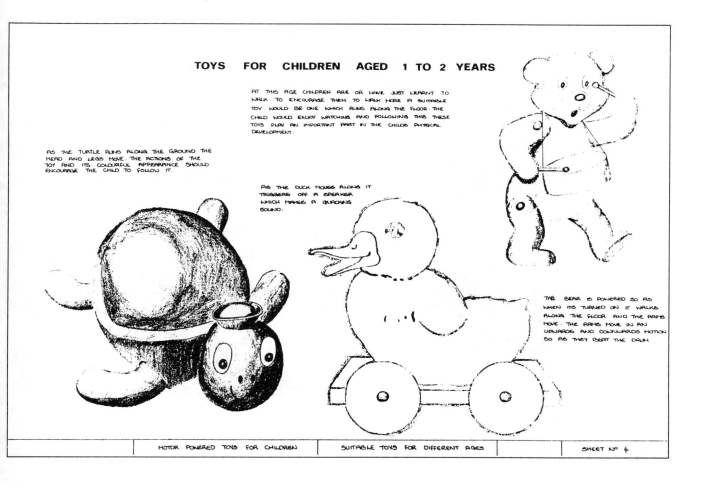

AT THIS AGE CHILDREN ARE OR HAVE JUST LEARNT TO WALK. TO ENCOURAGE THEM TO WALK MORE A SUITABLE TOY WOULD BE ONE WHICH RUNS ALONG THE FLOOR. THE CHILD WOULD ENJOY WATCHING AND FOLLOWING THIS. THESE TOYS PLAY AN IMPORTANT PART IN THE CHILDS PHYSICAL DEVELOPMENT.

AS THE TURTLE RUNS ALONG THE GROUND THE HEAD AND LEGS MOVE. THE ACTIONS OF THE TOY AND ITS COLOURFUL APPEARANCE SHOULD ENCOURAGE THE CHILD TO FOLLOW IT.

AS THE DUCK MOVES ALONG IT TRIGGERS OFF A SPEAKER WHICH MAKES A QUACKING SOUND.

THE BEAR IS POWERED SO AS WHEN ITS TURNED ON IT WALKS ALONG THE FLOOR AND THE ARMS MOVE. THE ARMS MOVE IN AN UPWARDS AND DOWNWARDS MOTION SO AS THEY BEAT THE DRUM

MOTOR POWERED TOYS FOR CHILDREN	SUITABLE TOYS FOR DIFFERENT AGES		SHEET Nº 4

TOYS   FOR   CHILDREN   AGED   2 TO 3 YEARS

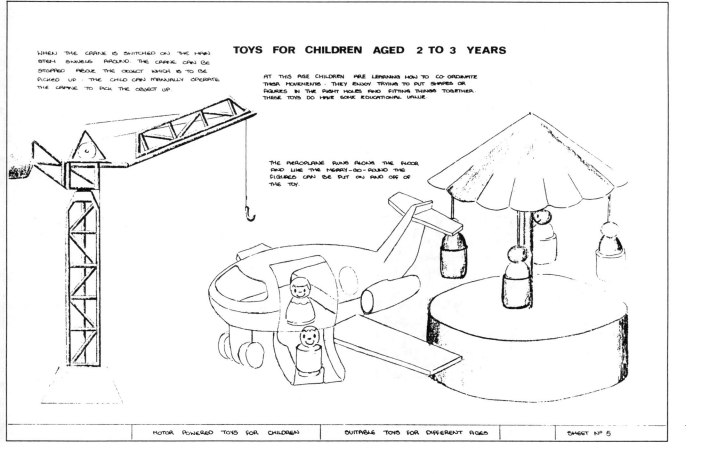

WHEN THE CRANE IS SWITCHED ON THE MAIN STEM SWIVELS AROUND. THE CRANE CAN BE STOPPED ABOVE THE OBJECT WHICH IS TO BE PICKED UP. THE CHILD CAN MANUALLY OPERATE THE CRANE TO PICK THE OBJECT UP.

AT THIS AGE CHILDREN ARE LEARNING HOW TO CO-ORDINATE THEIR MOVEMENTS. THEY ENJOY TRYING TO PUT SHAPES OR FIGURES IN THE RIGHT HOLES AND FITTING THINGS TOGETHER. THESE TOYS DO HAVE SOME EDUCATIONAL VALUE.

THE AEROPLANE RUNS ALONG THE FLOOR AND LIKE THE MERRY-GO-ROUND THE FIGURES CAN BE PUT ON AND OFF OF THE TOY.

MOTOR POWERED TOYS FOR CHILDREN	SUITABLE TOYS FOR DIFFERENT AGES		SHEET Nº 5

TOYS FOR CHILDREN AGED 3 TO 5 YEARS

CHILDREN AT THIS AGE ARE STARTING TO USE THEIR IMAGINATION. PRETENDING TO BE A PILOT WHILE PLAYING WITH THEIR HELICOPTER OR A RACING CAR DRIVER IN THEIR TOY CAR. THESE TYPES OF TOYS HAVE REALLY ONLY A PLAY VALUE AND ARE NOT EDUCATIONAL.

BOTH THE ROTARY BLADES ON TOP OF THE HELICOPTER AND ON THE TAIL FIN ROTATE WHEN SWITCHED ON

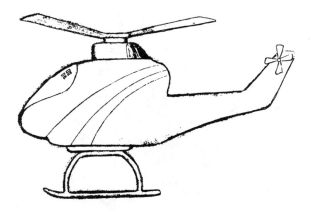

| MOTOR POWERED TOYS FOR CHILDREN | SUITABLE TOYS FOR DIFFERENT AGES | | SHEET Nº 6 |

Project Title

Motor driven toy

Summary of Design Brief

Age of user to be decided, toy should be safe to use and appealing to play with. All electrical parts to be contained within toy. Access should be included so as to change battery. No major restrictions on materials or size.

Evaluation

When the toy was finished I found that the motor wasn't powerfull enough to push it along. When pushed along the movements of the toy worked but not as well as they could.

The first problem that I had while constructing the toy was the head. At first the cam wouldn't push the head out it kept getting stuck so I applied plenty of wax which helped. When the head was comming out the elastic band wouldn't pull it back in again. So I tryed attatching the elastic band to different places until I found the best one. It worked here but it could have been better if the elastic band was stronger.

The second problem was with the legs, they wouldn't sit on the cams properly. So I had to keep on adjusting the position which they were stuck. The appertures in the top shell also had to be cut wider and higher as the legs were not clearing the shell. The same had to be done with the bottom appertures as the cams were hitting the shell.

If the motor was powerful enough to push the toy, then it could be operated by a young child. But I don't think that its that suitable as its not strong enough.

If designing it again I would use stronger plastics especially for the head which is polystyrene. Also the way in which the head and legs work would have to be thought about more.

| MOTOR POWERED TOYS FOR CHILDREN | SUITABLE TOYS FOR DIFFERENT AGES | | SHEET Nº 7 |

WHAT USE HAD BEEN MADE OF LOCAL RESOURCES?

This is what the assessor would like to know next. It would have been helpful if a comment or two had been made. It would be nice to think that much of the work in the Folio came as a result of primary investigation, i.e. *personal observations*. The teacher would know this, but the assessor would have to make an enquiry before being able to complete the moderation. The advice here is to *write a list of local resources*, such as children at home, local playgroup, local library, etc. Where information on mechanisms and electronics has come from books, it would be helpful to know the titles and page numbers.

HOW WELL IS THE INFORMATION RECORDED AND ORGANISED?

Since this Folio is easy to read, and the sheets are numbered, then this must rate as a very well-presented Research and Investigation Folio.

IS THE DETAIL APPROPRIATE AND DEALT WITH IN SUFFICIENT DEPTH?

The answer to this must be that the research and investigation was appropriate and the depth of detail just adequate for the problem. Had there been *more* evidence of research into the effect of colour, texture, material and safety, this would have been an example of an excellent Research and Investigation Folio.

THE EVALUATION

The evaluation of the completed toy was done after the Design and Answer Sheets had been completed. The design was realised and then placed in the Folio ready for the teacher to assess as part of the coursework.

The evaluation is mainly concerned with constructional problems and it would appear that there was insufficient time for it to be ready for testing with a child. However, it was helpful to see that design problems of a technical nature were recognised and that recommendations were made for improvements. Had more time been available, or had the student been able to complete the task within the given time, then the evaluation could have included comments about the analysis of the problem written on sheet 1 of the Design Answer Sheets.

UNIT 7   REALISATION OF THE DESIGN

Your teacher will mark your work and will allocate marks for the areas involved in the making of a product. Again, the LEAG Design and Realisation marking scheme is used as an example, but the principles are relevant to the way all the Examining Groups mark realisation. Marks are allocated to the following areas of making:

Planning, organisation and completion of tasks	10 marks
Use of appropriate techniques	10 marks
End product: accuracy	10 marks
quality of finish	10 marks
Safe working procedures	10 marks
TOTAL	50 marks

To give your teacher guidance, the table below is provided so that a mark can be awarded for the following categories:

Superb	9–10
Highly satisfactory	7–8
Satisfactory	5–6
Slightly unsatisfactory	3–4
Unsatisfactory	0–2

So to get a 'superb' total mark it would be necessary for you to score between 9 and 10 marks in each of the making areas that are being assessed in the realisation.

7.1 How to get a 'superb' mark in the realisation

The following is a description of what is meant by 'superb' in the LEAG mark scheme. The principles are valid for all the Examining Groups.

For planning, organisation, and completion of tasks

> Organises working procedures in a logical sequence and successfully completes the artefact.

To be considered for a 'superb' mark, it is expected that the artefact, product, solution, etc. should be *completed*. If your work was complex and not completed, you could still be considered for a superb award. However, you are strongly recommended to consider the time that is available for making, and to try to produce a complete solution within that time.

For use of appropriate techniques and materials

> The quality of work reflects due care and precision in tool application resulting in a high level of craftsmanship. Correct use of techniques in relationship to the type of materials being used.

If the finished work is neat, and the surface treatment is of a high standard, then it is reasonable to assume that the correct method of production was used for the material or materials. The surfaces will tend to be free from scratch marks left by a saw or file, the corner edges would be free from arrises (sharp edges) and the general appearance would be of a high quality.

For accuracy

> Measurements on the artefact will match those on the drawing. A high level of precision will be shown in machine-produced components.

Accuracy in measurements is concerned with the precise length, thickness and width of materials. It is also concerned with the dimensions of straight, flat, rounded, angular, parallel and tapered shapes, and how well the various components fit together. Some components have tight fits, in which case the structure should be rigid, or sliding fits, in which case the components should slide smoothly and with very little 'play' or 'binding'.

For quality of finish

> Appropriate surface finish properly applied to a high standard. Evidence that the finish was obtained by careful and thorough work throughout each stage.

There are finishes that can be applied to a variety of materials and which therefore could be regarded as appropriate. However, the *function* of the product has to be considered; e.g. if the product is to be put in water, then it must have a waterproof finish. If a product is *not* exposed to water, moisture, etc., then there is no need for a waterproof finish if an appropriate non-waterproof finish is available.

To obtain a good finish with a varnish, polish, paint, etc., it is necessary to *prepare* the surface of the material very carefully. This may mean careful sanding, rubbing down, etc. *before* the first coat is applied, and rubbing down with a fine abrasive *in between* applying each coat. Of course there are materials such as acrylic, plastic laminates, and plastic-film-covered boards that do *not* require a finish treatment. In cases where these materials are used, the quality of finish is determined by the absence of unwanted marks, blemishes, etc. caused during the making of the solution. To use such materials and to complete the making without causing unwanted marks does require a high level of care and skill.

For safety

> Proficient and safe use of tools, machines and other workshop equipment. Would be able to work without supervision.

There are correct and incorrect ways of doing things in a workshop. The main reason being that some methods are safe and others are not. The correct ways also produce better quality results.

There are correct ways of *holding* materials in a lathe, on a drilling machine bed, in a vice, etc. If these are followed, then you are working safely.

The next aspect concerned with safety is your *clothing*. Are you wearing the necessary protective clothing for the work you are doing? Are you wearing a visor to protect your eyes when working on a lathe? Are you wearing a leather apron when working with hot metal?

These are just a few of the things a teacher will look for when assessing your ability to work safely. To be trusted to work on your own without close supervision is an indication that you *can* be relied upon to apply all the safety regulations and procedures and to adopt a common-sense approach to working in a workshop.

7.2 How to get a 'satisfactory' mark in the realisation

The following is a description of what is meant by 'satisfactory' (i.e. average) in the LEAG mark scheme. Again, the principles are valid for all the Examining Groups.

For planning, organisation, and completion of tasks

> Outlines working procedures in a brief form and completes artefact in some instances. Operations and processes may be out of sequence.

It is usually expected that an average candidate should have the parts fitted together and in a state where functioning parts can be demonstrated. Some parts may not be completed but at least the product is largely together. The *order* in which the parts were made may have been rather inefficient, with some time being wasted by having to wait for glue to harden or a paint to dry. Had the timing of the processes been better, more time could have been devoted to *completing* other tasks. It is often a good plan to complete a gluing or painting stage by the end of a lesson. Then, when you return for the next lesson, the glue will have hardened and/or the paint will have dried and you will be able to continue working. 'Careful planning helps to get work completed on time.'

For use of appropriate techniques and materials

> Shows an ability to use a limited range of tools but the resulting standard of craftsmanship may lack precision and crispness. At the upper end of this category there will be some evidence to show that appropriate constructional techniques have been applied.

The limited range of *tools* used may be dictated by the limited range of *materials* used. In addition to this limitation, imposed by the choice of materials, an average student would not necessarily be expected to use fully the range of tools still available. However, at least at the upper end of the average mark range, candidates should be able to use the appropriate constructional techniques for any given material. For example, constructions made from wood could be assembled using nails, glue, screws, and using joints such as mortice and tenon, dowelling, housing, halving, and some dovetail joints. For constructions made of metal, candidates at the upper end of the mark range should be able to join metal by rivetting, tapping and threading, soldering, brazing and welding.

For accuracy

> Overall dimensions generally conform to those given on the working drawing, but there will be some inaccuracy in detail.

This inaccuracy often shows itself where parts are *joined*. They may not meet up exactly; some joints that should be rigid are slack; right-angled corners are not at 90°; parallel surfaces are not parallel; and sliding fits do not run smoothly. Or there may be a variation in lengths, widths and thicknesses that should be the same.

For quality of finish

On a completed artefact, a finishing process has been applied but inexpertly. Where the artefact is not complete, there will be signs that an attempt has been made to apply a suitable finish to individual items.

The average student often finds that he or she has allowed too little time for this process. This means that it has to be done in a hurry, so some parts do not get treated. Those that are treated receive less care than is necessary, and the finished result is not as good as it might be.

For safety

Shows a regard for the need for safe working practices. Normally follows the rules for safety, but needs guidance at times.

Often the average candidate forgets to follow some of the safe working practices and risks having an accident or damaging the work. A reminder from the teacher is sometimes necessary to stop such risks being taken.

7.3 How to get an 'unsatisfactory' mark in the realisation

The following is a description of what is meant by 'unsatisfactory' in the LEAG mark scheme. The principles are valid for all Examining Groups.

For planning, organisation, and completion of tasks

Produces very little in the way of working procedures. Processes will often be out of sequence. Some stages of the construction will be attempted but the artefact will not be completed.

Unfinished work is typical of weak candidates. Some parts may have been shaped and even been given a finish, but it is rare for a weak candidate to have the parts assembled. The fact that very little time, if any, is devoted to planning often shows itself in the candidate not knowing what is to be done next. Weak candidates often rely upon the teacher to tell him or her what the next stage should be. If the teacher then says, 'you tell me what you should be doing next', the candidate either makes a few wild guesses or remains silent because he or she does not know the answer. Such a candidate often has periods with no productive work and looks around to see what others are doing. The candidate's own work is therefore incomplete.

For the use of appropriate techniques and materials

Will be able to attempt, with a little success, some of the basic processes needed to complete the artefact.

This means that there will be little *evidence* in the work to show that an artefact has been well made. Basic processes, such as nailing, will show poor alignment of the pieces being joined and hammer marks in the materials. There may even be signs that a nail has penetrated through a side where it was not intended.

For accuracy

There will be some resemblance to the original drawing in form rather than in size. Assembly may not be possible due to inaccurate work.

It should still be possible to see that the drawing and the material prepared are connected. The outline on the drawing is similar, even if it is not the same size, as the shaped piece of material. Because the parts are not accurately marked out and not cut at the correct angle, some parts will not fit together.

For quality of finish

Little evidence of any final finish being applied to the components.

Because the candidate has not been able to fit the parts together, it is possible that the work is not ready for a finish to be applied. So no attempt may have been made to complete this task.

For safety

Applies safety rules to the use of basic hand tools but requires constant supervision and guidance when using other equipment in the workshop.

The weak candidate needs a lot of the teacher's attention when using equipment such as a lathe, injection moulding machine, brazing torch, etc.
Where do *you* fit in these three categories?

You can think about your own experience in the workshop and see how *you* compare with the three categories that have been outlined by the Examining Group. You may find that in some aspects you appear to be outstanding and in others just above average. Or you may find that you fit into all three categories in different aspects. It is however more likely that for some of the aspects you fit somewhere in between the categories.

As you can see from the mark schemes of the Northern Examining Association below, many of the principles we have considered for *realisation* apply in a similar fashion in other Examining Groups.

N E A :   R E A L I S A T I O N
A S S E S S M E N T   S H E E T

Manufacturing a) **Construction** Workmanship. A range of appropriate techniques	Not submitted (if no realisation is submitted no grade will be determined)	ABS
	Simple or inappropriate construction showing few techniques and/or a poor standard of workmanship	1–10
	EITHER A limited range of simple or appropriate techniques, but showing a good standard of workmanship *OR* a larger range of more complex techniques showing a poor standard of workmanship	11–20
	A wide range of more complex, sound, constructional techniques showing a high level of workmanship	21–30
b) **Accuracy** In relation to working drawing and constructional details	Little accuracy	0–2
	Overall dimensions generally accurate, some details not as planned	3–6
	A high degree of accuracy with all details as planned	7–10
c) **Finish**	No surface finish or inappropriate finishes	0–2
	Appropriate surface finishes, but details of limited quality	3–6
	High standard of appropriate finish to all materials	7–10
d) **Aesthetic Quality** Judgement of appearance, function and suitability for its environment	Poor appearance, unsuitable for function or its environment	0–2
	Generally suitable but limited in some details	3–6
	Appearance and function highly suitable for its environment	7–10
e) **Applied Knowledge** Transfer of design proposal into planned sequence of actions. Correct use of appropriate tools, techniques and processes	Supervision of all work needed	0–2
	Understands general use of tool techniques and processes but some guidance needed	3–6
	Most realisation processes planned and executed with little guidance	7–10
	MANUFACTURING SUB-TOTAL	70
	ADJUSTED DESIGN SUB-TOTAL (Divided by 3)	30
	PROJECT TOTAL	100

EXAMPLES OF STUDENT COURSEWORK

Just as there are many solutions to a single problem, so there are many different ways of presenting the information that leads up to the making of a product. And although there are differences among the Examining Groups, there is a *structure* that is common to all the assignments which involve solving a problem. The structure shown in Fig 4.1 has been called the *designing process*.

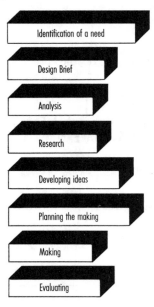

Fig 4.1
The designing process

It is important therefore that these areas are easily identified in your work. Remember, all the coursework you are doing has two important aims. The first is *solving problems* and the second is *getting a good grade* in the subject.

▶ The first aim is achieved by completing all the tasks involved in designing.
▶ The second aim is achieved by presenting all the information clearly for someone to assess.

You will see from the examples in this chapter that the quality of presentation does vary; in some it is easy to follow and understand, in others much less so. The *comments* that accompany each example of coursework highlight some of the points you should bear in mind in your own work.

UNIT 1 DESIGNING FOR THE NEEDS OF THE DISABLED AND HANDICAPPED

1.1 Problem set by WJEC (assessment weighting 25%)

Not all equipment for the disabled and the handicapped needs to be elaborate or expensive. Many people can be helped by using simple, inexpensive, purpose-built aids designed to overcome their specific difficulties.

Either a) A personal aid

With the advice of your teacher, contact a local person (or the parents of a child) who is physically disabled, infirm, blind, deaf or in some way handicapped. With the assistance of the disabled person, design and build a piece of equipment that will help him/her overcome his/her individual disability or in some way improve the quality of his/her life.

Or b) An aid for more general use

With the advice of your teacher, contact a local charity or some other organisation that helps disabled or handicapped people. With the assistance of that organisation, design and build a piece of equipment that can be used by the disabled or handicapped.

The equipment may be fixed or portable, it may be for use in the home or centre for the disabled or in a more public place, e.g. at a local beauty spot or at the shops.

1.2 Student's answer

Contents:

	Contents	Sheet No 1		

Situation:

My aged grandfather, of sound mind and health, lost his left leg in the war and is now finding it increasingly more of a struggle to move around by the conventional means of an artificial leg. A walking stick would remedy the situation but an injury incurred at the same time will not permit any weight to be put on his right elbow.

	Situation	Sheet No. 2		

Specification:

Designing for the needs of the disabled and the handicapped.

Not all equipment for the disabled and handicapped needs to be elaborate or expensive. Many people can be helped by using simple, inexpensive purpose-built aids designed to overcome their specific difficulties.

Either (a) A Personal Aid.

With the advice of your teacher, contact a local person (or the parents of a child) who is physically disabled, infirm, blind, deaf or in some other way handicapped. With the assistance of the disabled person, design and build a piece of equipment that will help him/her overcome his/her individual disability or in some way improve the quality of his or her life.

Or (b) An Aid for more General Use.

With the advice of your teacher, contact a local charity or some other organisation that helps disabled or handicapped people. With the assistance of a person from that organisation, design and build a piece of equipment that can be used by the disabled or handicapped.

The equipment may be fixed or portable, it may be for use in the home or centre for the disabled or in a more public place eg. at a local beauty spot or at the shops etc.

Applied Specification:

Within the limitations of reasonable cost and nine months' working time, I am to design and construct a walking stick substitute to the individual requirements of my grandfather, which will allow comfortable walking, as his unfortunate accumulation of injuries represent a quite unique disabled situation.

	Specification	Sheet No. 3		

Investigation:

Brôn-y-Nant (20:06:86)

Brôn-y-Nant is a short or long term stay, voluntary day home for the physically and mentally handicapped. Situated in a relatively picturesque part of Mochdre, it has recently benefited from the addition of an aviary presented by pupils of Rydal School using the CDT centre. As a school, we are therefore on favourable terms with the home and their help in researching this particular field of investigation has been much appreciated and useful, whether or not it provides a direct stimulus for design.

Before commencing, the point was emphasized to us that the home catered for 18 to 60 year olds with various disorders, including psychiatric illnesses such as schizophrenia; though they may appear peculiar to us and have a low IQ. they are, and thus require, the respect of an adult.

Instantly striking was the overwhelming atmosphere of gratuitous smoking in every room. Several rooms have been allocated for general use, where kitchen equipment is included supervisional guidance may well be necessary. To allow some degree of privacy, injections etc. are carried out behind locked doors.

Their main enemy is the prejudice of the general public – the stereotyped image coupled with an unwillingnes to accept them into society. In an attempt to combat this vicious circle, the residents at the home are encouraged to wash and shave – it is considered a matter of some importance that the atmosphere is as homely and relaxed as possible so the contrast with society is less striking; there are no uniforms etc. to distinguish staff and patients. Similarly, they are given facilities to knit and paint, some artwork being of an excellent standard. Previously, the 'students', as they are preferably known as, had to pay for the convenience, but now the facilities are supplied free of charge, largely to encourage personal hygiene.

Mental disorders frequently apply only in certain fields, allowing them to excel in others. Nevertheless, being partially retarded was sufficient to condemn them to a life in which they were taken from their family to attend a special school then subsequently this day centre, therefore their whole life has been spent amongst people such as themselves. Just as we do, they emulate those around them so the emphasis is to get out, circulate within the community and utilise such facilities as the sports centre, so they might change and thereby be more acceptable to us.

Financial resources being low, the sparse staff struggle to prepare meals for some 30 patients daily, of which they try to maintain a balance · 15 handicapped and 15 with an illness of some sort. The local physiotherapist regularly visits the centre, her job is to analyze the specific problem, and relate ideas to the individual. Amongst her suggested specifications for educational aids were : jigsaws – bell rings if right ; balancing devices, possibly weighted which could allow for adaption ; co-ordination stimulating apparatus ; lights to encourage eye movement. Of particular interest was the case of a certain patient who had now recovered from an accident but refused to use the arm he had injured as it had proved a source of attention. Therefore, a switch for TV games, which could for future use be adapted for elbow or foot control, might help remedy this particular situation.

	Investigation	Sheet No. 4		

Investigation:

As a matter of primary research, copies of the letter opposite were despatched to the following fourteen different organisations, between the dates of July 23 and September 13, 1986. :-

* THE ARTHRITIS AND RHEUMATISM COUNCIL, 41 Eagle Street, London WC1R 4AR.
ARTHRITIS CARE, 6 Grosvenor Crescent, London SW1S 7ER.
* THE DHSS STORE, Health Publications Unit, Heywood, Lancs. OL10 2PZ.
* INSTITUTE OF CONSUMER ERGONOMICS, University of Technology, Leics. LE11 0JB.
* VISITING AIDS CENTRE, 16 Fitzroy Square, London W1P 5HQ.
NOTTINGHAM MEDICAL AIDS, P.O. Box 96, Nottingham NG2 6HE.
* DISABLED LIVING FOUNDATION'S INFORMATION SERVICE, 380/384 Harrow Rd, London W9.
* MECANAIDS LTD., Gloucester, GL1 1BR.
AREMCO, Grove House, Lenham, Kent ME17 2PX.
* CAMP LTD., Portfield Ind. Estate, Nevil Shute Rd., Portsmouth, Hants.
* HOMECRAFT SUPPLIES, 27 Trinity Road, London SW17 7SF.
LLEWELLYN & CO. LTD., Carlton Works, Carlton Street, Liverpool L3 7ED.
* HUGH STEEPER (ORANGE AIDS), 237/239 Roehampton Lane, London SW15 4LB.
NORAN AIDS, 89 Humber Road, Beeston, Notts. NG9 2ET.

Replies were received from those marked. Obviously, some were more helpful than others - 'CAMP LTD' being worthy of particular note, they have since received a note of thanks for their generous contribution. Similarly, some material was of no use so, for ease of reference, a collection of the relative resource material was compiled in a seperate compendium.

David Pritchard Howarth,
5 Princes Drive,
Colwyn Bay,
N. Wales.
LL29 8LH.
23 July 1986.

Dear Sir/Madam,

My reason for writing to you is that, as an O-level student, my chosen assignment for CDT is to design either a personal or wide range use piece of equipment which will assist the disabled and handicapped overcome everyday difficulties. As I am sure you will understand, the research and investigation forms the backbone and is of immense importance to the successful completion of such a project, and needs to be compiled now.

Therefore, your kind assistance in supplying me with catologues, information booklets or pamplets, or anything else of a similar nature covering the wide scope of disability -mental and physical- describing the condition; its causes and effects; or previously designed and proven equipment, would be vastly appreciated.

If however you find yourself unable to comply with my request, then I thank you for having had the courtesy to read this letter.

Yours Faithfully,

Investigation   Sheet No. 5

Investigation:

Extension of Situation:

Mr. I.E. Jones had been trained in telecommunication techniques and so, at the outbreak of the second World War, he was enrolled in the Signals and assigned to the 50th. division, 8th. Army.

During the advance on Sicily, south-west of Catania, Mr. Jones was driving an equipment truck which came under heavy mortar fire. Swerving to avoid the shrapnel, the lorry was blown up by a mine - the driver receiving the full impact of the blast.

This unfortunate accident had tragic consequences on Mr. Jones' future - he lost an eye, had a compound fracture of the right elbow; and as a result of the mine, an upper-thigh amputation of the left leg was necessary.

As a member of the 'British Limbless Ex-Service Men's Association, Mr. Jones has been provided with a relatively sophisticated artificial leg which is nevertheless awkward and sometimes painful to wear, but he has still, till now, managed to amble around unaided. He has tried unsuccessfully to use a walking stick because the lower tip of his humerus had shattered meaning that his right arm would never again be capable of handling any weight. Also, the 'casualty clearing station' in Sicily could only set the bone allowing minimal movement - though previous life had included some time as an army P.E. instructor he was now to be restricted to a desk job.

Even in this capacity, Mr. Jones worked his way up through the ranks of the GPO from a technical officer to an inspector, all the way to an executive when he retired some years ago.

Investigation   Sheet No. 6

Investigation:

Ergonomics:

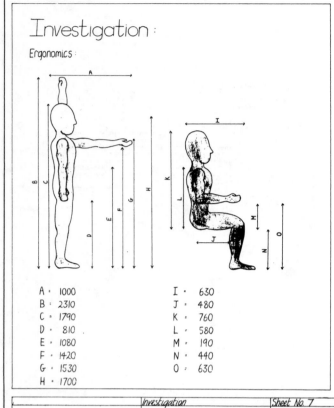

A = 1000	I = 630
B = 2310	J = 480
C = 1790	K = 760
D = 810	L = 580
E = 1080	M = 190
F = 1420	N = 440
G = 1530	O = 630
H = 1700	

Major Muscles involved:

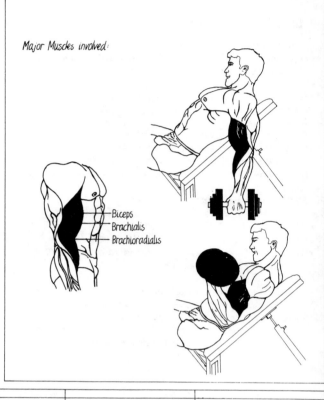

- Biceps
- Brachialis
- Brachioradialis

		Investigation		Sheet No. 7		

Investigation:

Whatever solution I come up with, it is essential to know, with some accuracy, the complete range of movement of my grandfather's right arm. Laterally, movement is hardly restricted, the angle of pivot of his elbow does however represent a limitation and needs to be measured.

To do this a large protractor-type device is needed. As I do not have access to such an instrument I must make a simple substitute.

(See Camp Ltd. folder '1984-85 catalogue p. 4)

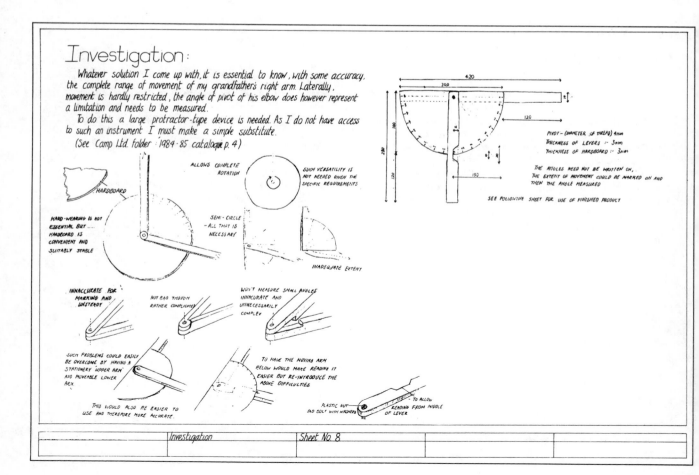

ALLOWS COMPLETE ROTATION

SUCH VERSATILITY IS NOT NEEDED GIVEN THE SPECIFIC REQUIREMENTS

HARDBOARD

HARD-WEARING IS NOT ESSENTIAL BUT HARDBOARD IS CONVENIENT AND SUITABLY STABLE

SEMI-CIRCLE - ALL THAT IS NECESSARY

INADEQUATE EXTENT

INACCURATE FOR MARKING AND UNSTEADY

NOT BAD THOUGH RATHER COMPLICATED

WON'T MEASURE SMALL ANGLES INACCURATE AND UNNECESSARILY COMPLEX

SUCH PROBLEMS COULD EASILY BE OVERCOME BY HAVING A STATIONARY UPPER ARM AND MOVEABLE LOWER ARM

TO HAVE THE MOVING ARM BELOW WOULD MAKE READING IT EASIER BUT RE-INTRODUCE THE ABOVE DIFFICULTIES

THIS WOULD ALSO BE EASIER TO USE AND THEREFORE MORE ACCURATE.

PLASTIC NUT AND BOLT WITH WASHERS

TO ALLOW READING FROM MIDDLE OF LEVER

PIVOT - (DIAMETER OF THREAD) 4mm
THICKNESS OF LEVERS :- 3mm
THICKNESS OF HARDBOARD :- 3mm

THE ANGLES NEED NOT BE WRITTEN ON, THE EXTENT OF MOVEMENT COULD BE MARKED ON AND THEN THE ANGLE MEASURED

SEE FOLLOWING SHEET FOR USE OF FINISHED PRODUCT

		Investigation		Sheet No. 8		

Investigation:

Limb Movement: (For movement of the arm ; see following page for diagram).

The biceps contracts and shortens, pulling on the radius. The scapula holds firm so the lower arm is pulled up. The triceps is antagonistic (acts in opposition) to the biceps, and is relaxed, so it lengthens. The brachialis muscle (see previous page) also works antagonistically to the triceps. When the triceps contracts , the biceps relaxes and the arm extends.

Applied Research of Arm Movement:

Mr. Jones' actual muscles do not themselves represent the problem ; though withered through age and inhibited use. The restricted arm movement is a direct consequence of the ball of his 'humerus' bone being shattered , it is therefore unable to pivot freely within the socket (the 'olecranon process').

	Investigation	Sheet No. 9		

Investigation:

Antagonistic Muscles of Forearm:

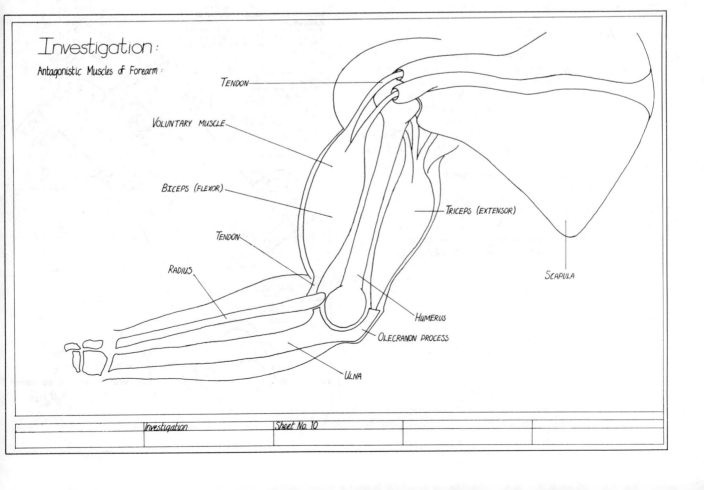

TENDON
VOLUNTARY MUSCLE
BICEPS (FLEXOR)
TENDON
RADIUS
TRICEPS (EXTENSOR)
SCAPULA
HUMERUS
OLECRANON PROCESS
ULNA

	Investigation	Sheet No. 10		

Investigation:

Functional requirements of the aid:

SUPPORT - This is imperative to attain from the start. The aid must be capable of supporting his bodyweight.

THERAPEUTIC - Though Mr. Jones' disability is beyond cure, the aid is to allow - or preferably encourage - walking in a normal or near normal manner.

PREVENTATIVE - An attempt to prevent or further prevent postural deformities occuring through muscular un-balance by more even bodyweight distribution while walking, and to some extent it ought to relieve the pain of the artificial leg and its shoulder strap.

Other requirements to be considered:

COMFORT - The prolonged use of the aid means that it must not cause any pain or discomfort, either directly or indirectly by placing pressure on his right elbow.

CONVENIENCE - The apparatus should be simple and easy to use, as light as possible, easily stored, and completely safe.

APPEARANCE - Mr Jones' personal preference is that the aid be attractive yet as unobtrusive as possible.

CONFIDENCE - It is important that the aid be light and compact from the point of view of practicality, but Mr. Jones is a fairly hefty gentleman so it must be heavy and sturdy enough to allow a sense of security, and confidence that the apparatus can support his weight. It may be an essentially psychological consideration but it is imperative my grandfather feel at ease with the aid.

STABILITY - With the wide variety of different-textured surfaces encountered frequently within everyday life a sure grip, providing maximum stability, is a very important safety factor.

	Investigation	Sheet No. 11		

Investigation:

Through careful study of the resource material and consultation with my grandfather, two distinctly different realms of investigation leading to potential solutions become apparent.

Firstly, some sort of mechanical device which would clamp onto the arm, locking it in position so as to allow normal use of a walking stick - the pressure which would ordinarily have been placed on the elbow, under such circumstances would be partly absorbed by the aid, and partly transferred to the stronger upper-arm. (See opposite and Camp Ltd. folder: Upper and Lower Limb orthoses and the "NuKO" booklet. See also following sheet.)

Secondly, the more obvious, if somewhat cumbersome, solution of a walking stick/crutch variation which would take all possible pressure completely away from the arm. (See 2nd following sheet, taken from Camp Ltd. folder: 1984-85 catalogue, p. 30-31.)

The two ideas ought to be developed seperately and the two solutions obtained compared and even possibly combined to select the best solution.

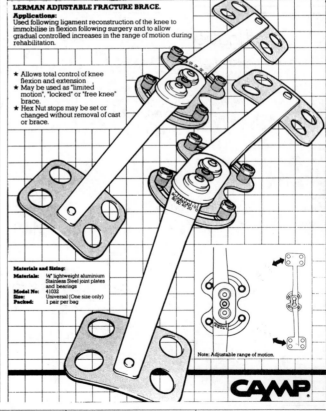

LERMAN ADJUSTABLE FRACTURE BRACE.
Applications:
Used following ligament reconstruction of the knee to immobilise in flexion following surgery and to allow gradual controlled increases in the range of motion during rehabilitation.

★ Allows total control of knee flexion and extension
★ May be used as "limited motion", "locked" or "free knee" brace.
★ Hex Nut stops may be set or changed without removal of cast or brace.

Materials and Sizing:
Materials: ¼" lightweight aluminium Stainless Steel joint plates and bearings
Model No: 41032
Size: Universal (One size only)
Packed: 1 pair per bag

Note: Adjustable range of motion.

CAMP.

	Investigation	Sheet No. 12		

Sheets 13–18 continued the investigation of the earlier sheets.

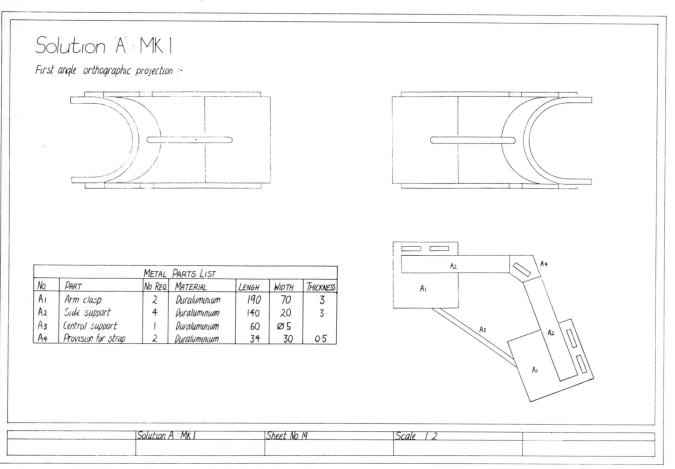

Solution 'A' : MK I

First angle orthographic projection :-

No.	PART	No REQ.	MATERIAL	LENGH	WIDTH	THICKNESS
A1	Arm clasp	2	Duraluminium	190	70	3
A2	Side support	4	Duraluminium	140	20	3
A3	Central support	1	Duraluminium	60	Ø 5	
A4	Provision for strap	2	Duraluminium	34	30	0·5

METAL PARTS LIST

Solution A : MK I	Sheet No. 19	Scale 1 2

Investigation:

Upon further consultation with my grandfather and teacher, possible improvements on 'Solution A : Mk I' have become apparent. The following modifications reduce amount of material and therefore also cost, and construction will be easier while maintaining all its original strength. As sheet No. 16 shows, metal supports are much stronger under compression than tension – a fact which warranted the inclusion of a straight rod, from forearm to bicep. However, this has been proven impossible in that it will not allow clothes to be worn over it, and I am convinced the alternative; shown below and taken from Sheet No. 15 of original ideas, No. 8, will provide more than adequate support strength.

Probably the most important modification is the change of material – steel has been chosen in preference to duraluminium for its strength qualities which mean less material needs to be used and the overall weight difference is negligable. Also, cold, countersunk rivets have replaced welding as the method of joining – no distortion will occur; it is easier, it gives a totally flush surface; and despite weakening the material in theory, it has been tested on 3mm steel, and it does provide a very strong join.

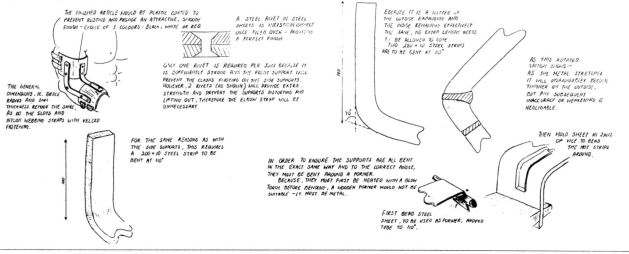

Investigation	Sheet No. 20		

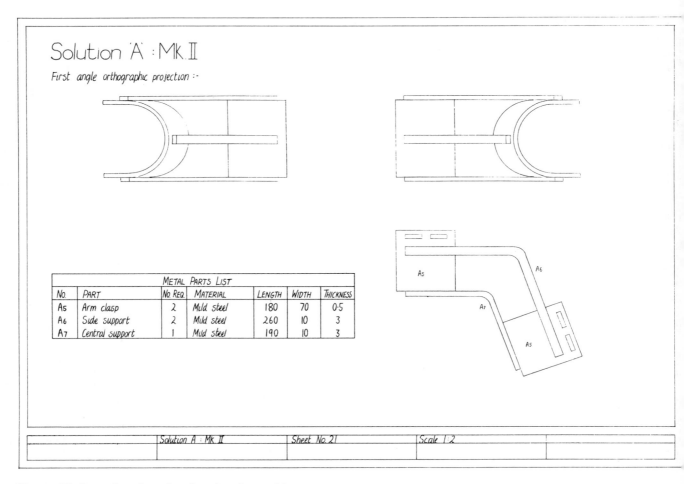

Solution 'A' : Mk.II

First angle orthographic projection :-

	METAL PARTS LIST					
No.	PART	No. REQ.	MATERIAL	LENGTH	WIDTH	THICKNESS
A5	Arm clasp	2	Mild steel	180	70	0·5
A6	Side support	2	Mild steel	260	10	3
A7	Central support	1	Mild steel	190	10	3

	Solution A : Mk II	Sheet No. 21	Scale 1:2	

Sheets 22–9 continued to develop the chosen idea.

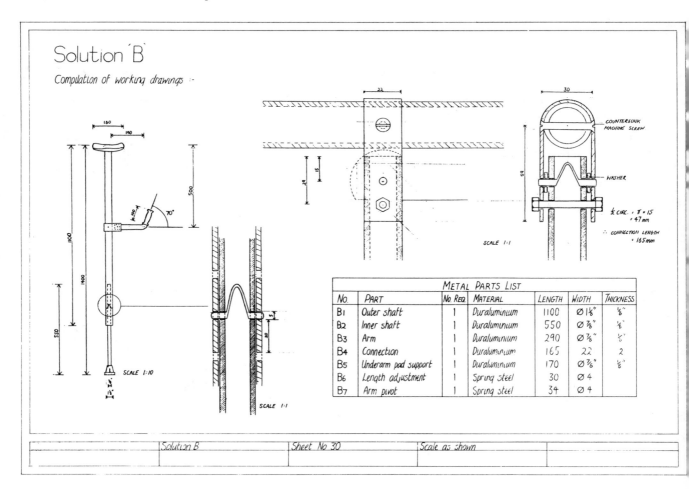

Solution 'B'

Compilation of working drawings :-

	METAL PARTS LIST					
No.	PART	No. REQ	MATERIAL	LENGTH	WIDTH	THICKNESS
B1	Outer shaft	1	Duraluminium	1100	Ø1⅛"	⅛"
B2	Inner shaft	1	Duraluminium	550	Ø⅞"	⅛"
B3	Arm	1	Duraluminium	290	Ø⅜"	½"
B4	Connection	1	Duraluminium	165	22	2
B5	Underarm pad support	1	Duraluminium	170	Ø⅞"	⅛"
B6	Length adjustment	1	Spring steel	30	Ø4	
B7	Arm pivot	1	Spring steel	34	Ø4	

	Solution B	Sheet No 30	Scale as shown	

Solution ´B´

Two-point perspective projection :-

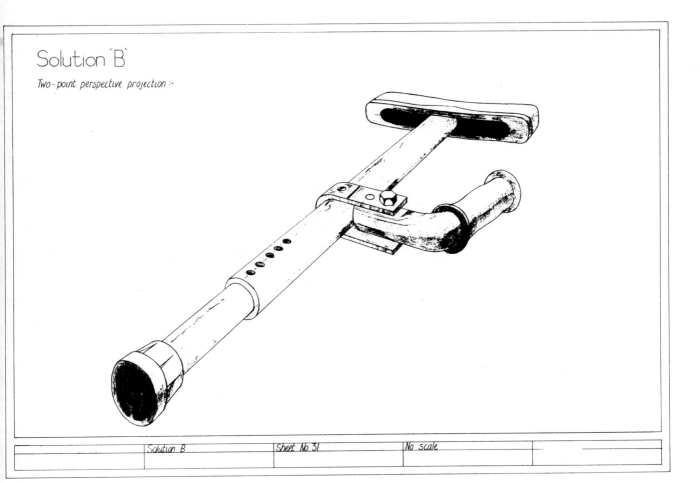

	Solution B	Sheet No. 31	No scale	

Selection :

With reference to the identification of likely problems involved ` (Sheet No. 15), the relative suitabilities of Solution A Mk Ⅱ and Solution B must be compared according to the various specified requirements. I believe both solutions are feasible – within my abilities, and restrictions of workshop and time. Moreover, I am sure either one would relieve my grandfather's situation.

SUPPORT – This imperative characteristic is unquestioned with the crutch, and all consulted sources agree that the 3mm steel supports of the arm brace are sufficient to absorb my grandfather's bodyweight.

THERAPEUTIC – Unfortunately neither solution allows walking in a completely normal manner, though the arm brace would permit near normal walking.

PREVENTATIVE – Obviously this is closely connected with the previous requirement ; muscular balance would be maintained through normal walking technique, therefore any postural deformities would be minimised most efficiently by use of the arm brace.

COMFORT – Solution B would be supremely comfortable ; despite underlying cloth there is always the possibility of the clasps pinching the skin or the necessarily tight straps causing some soreness.

CONVENIENCE – Both are simple and easy to use but Solution A Mk Ⅱ is much lighter and less obtrusive. The crutch can fold quite small but is nevertheless uncomparable, in this aspect, to the arm brace.

APPEARANCE – The arm brace itself is concealed beneath a shirt sleeve to allow use of a walking stick, any crutch inevitably emphasises disability.

CONFIDENCE – As previously stated, it is believed both solutions are strong enough, however, the crutch would undoubtedly provide a much greater sense of security – it is more obviously capable of withstanding his bodyweight.

STABILITY – With Solution A this is reliant on my grandfather's choice of walking stick. The crutch tip of Solution B is designed specifically for maximum stability.

The majority of the above factors support the selection of Solution A Mk Ⅱ, also my grandfather has expressed preference of, and confidence in, this solution.

	Selection	Sheet No. 32		

Investigation:

Further development of Solution A · Mk II

Even at this stage of development, modifications, to basically the same design, can be made. While the supports themselves remain 3mm steel, this has been replaced by sheet steel for the clasps which need not be particularly strong – this is cheaper, lighter and equally efficient. This does however introduce difficulties as regards joining support to clasp, obviously countersunk rivets cannot be used – the joint would be far too weak – as a flush surface is important, the only remaining alternative is hot joining, the most suitable form of which is brazing. This method was originally dismissed when duraluminium was to be used, because of its extremely coherent oxide layer, but this does not apply to steel. However, care must still be taken to ensure no distortion occurs – an especially relevant consideration now sheet steel is to be used, as this will heat up very quickly.

Requirements of finish are – smooth tactile qualities, durable, hygienic and of uniform, white, colour. It will frequently be worn beneath a white shirt so this colour is least noticeable, it must be smooth to touch otherwise it could catch the shirt – similarly, durability would restrict any blemishes incurred through everyday use. All the aforementioned are characteristics of 'plastic coating' using a powdered thermoplastic (see sheet No 41). It also provides complete protection against corrosion and reduces thermal conduction of artefact so it will not feel so 'cold', despite wearing a tube-grip type bandage beneath.

The final modification is a consequence of necessity rather than choice. On sheet No 18, it was decided that the straps would be made of nylon webbing because of its combination of flexibility and supreme strength, however, while this remains so, extensive search for such strapping of suitable width has proved futile. It is possible to cut 38mm strapping but, unless it is 'hot cut', the edges will fray – obviously unacceptable, and I do not have access to facilities to overcome this. Fortunately, a viable substitute has been found in 'cotton twill', folded double it is of comparable strength though it might give a little, it is however softer and more flexible.

Velcro is still to be the method of fastening for its ease of use yet great strength.

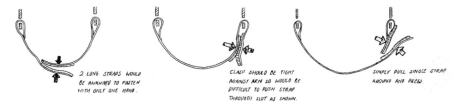

2 LONG STRAPS WOULD BE AWKWARD TO FASTEN WITH ONLY ONE HAND.

CLASP SHOULD BE TIGHT AGAINST ARM SO WOULD BE DIFFICULT TO PUSH STRAP THROUGH SLOT AS SHOWN.

SIMPLY PULL SINGLE STRAP AROUND AND PRESS.

	Investigation	Sheet No 33		

Solution 'A' · Mk II

Freehand isometric projection :-

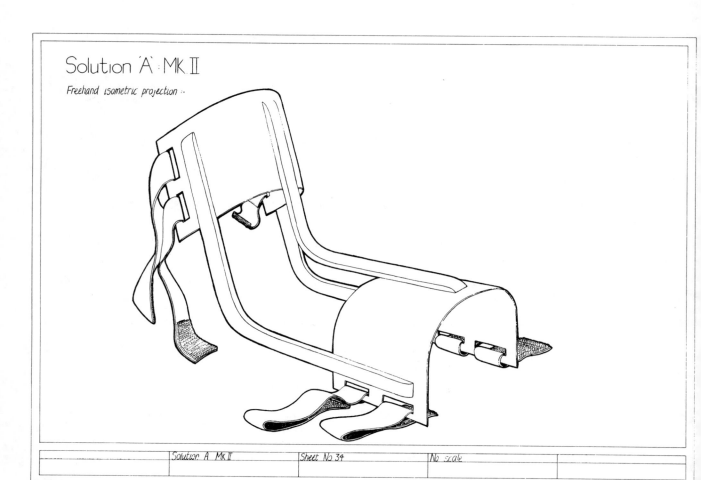

	Solution A Mk II	Sheet No 34	No scale	

Realisation

Sheets 35–44 completed a series of carefully selected photographs with annotations to explain the contents of each photograph. Below are two examples of the annotations.

The wooden former

This was a necessary tool from the start, the 83mm diameter is equivalent to that of my grandfather's lower and upper arm. It would therefore provide a 'dummy' about which the clasps may be bent, and the end is angled at 110° to assist when bending the supports.

Cutting out the arm clasps

Sheet steel is used because 3mm steel would be too expensive considering the clasps themselves need not be very strong. They are cut out using a 'notcher' for straight, accurate sides; the machine also guarantees perpendicular and parallel edges.

Evaluation:

During realisation it became apparent that from the origins of design I had made a fundamental error. Two arm measurements had been taken – upper and forearm circumferences. These two happened to be equal, and on this basis I mistakenly made the presumption that my grandfather's arm could be adequately represented by a cylinder of uniform diameter, this may be criticized within two specific criteria – the arm cross section is not a perfect circle; and whereas the upper arm circumference is relatively constant, the forearm varies considerably within the 70mm width of the arm clasp.

Although the situation may be remedied by wearing extra padding beneath the brace, this is neither comfortable or convenient. The only sure way of resolving this situation would have necessitated the prior construction of a cast mould of my grandfather's arm, from which accurate measurements may have been taken during the investigation and realisation processes. This does however remove the essential element of simplicity and gives rise to the question as to whether the entire design ought to be reviewed.

Nevertheless, my grandfather finds this serious error a minor inconvenience and of little consequence in terms of overall support – the fact that, using the arm brace, he is now able to use a walking stick and hence finds walking less painful, means the original specification has been satisfied. He was also very pleased with its smooth, clean finish – it has surpassed aesthetic requirements.

Nylon webbing may remain a suitable strap material, but there has been no appreciable weakness or stretching of the cotton twill used. Unfortunately however, both my grandfather and I were disappointed to discover that the actual strength of the velcro fasteners failed abysmally to fulfil our expectations, or indeed the manufacturer's claims. In retrospect it is agreed, the 'webbing style' ring fastener would have been preferable – perhaps more difficult to fasten, and maybe even less comfortable – but secure, (see sheet No. 18).

PATIENT'S EVALUATION

The aid, albeit designed to apply to my particular disability, offers many advantages:

The construction of this type of aid requires to be of lightweight composition, simple to manipulate and capable of withstanding the stresses exerted by the body weight.

It is therefore light in weight, of rigid construction, simple and efficient to operate. It is the simplicity, ease of attachment and manipulation, and the comfort offered in wearing the aid which gives the disabled person confidence and the assurance that he/she can depend upon the reliability of the support.

It is also appealing to find that apart from its practical function, it is also unobtrusive; can be worn under clothing without its presence being an embarrassment.

The finish is highly commendable; no discomfiture, does not restrict movement, and the absence of any rough edges adds to the enjoyment of the wearer.

If there is a weakness, it could perhaps be in the method of attachment. I would therefore suggest a single broader velcro strap on the upper and lower arm in lieu of the existing arrangement, and providing the elongated insertion apertures do not weaken the means of attachment.

I. E. JONES

| | Evaluation | Sheet No. 45 | | | |

Evaluation:

Several 'constructive criticisms' have evolved as to the improvement of the strap system, indicating insufficient thought and time were devoted to this aspect of design. These include abandoning velcro in favour of the 'webbing style' ring fastener, but even if velcro was retained, a single thick strap has been suggested in preference to the two seperate straps. This would allow a greater area of velcro overlap thus increasing its strength, however, this would also have the inevitable consequence of weakening the slot through which it is secured.

This problem may be halved by attaching the firm 'hook' velcro strip directly to the arm clasp using a contact adhesive such as Bostik Clear or Evostik. Such a method gives rise to another important yet previously unconsidered question — what is to be done when the straps became dirty? The present situation makes no provision for removal and washing, velcro may be washed on 'nylon' setting. Fortunately there is a relatively simple solution to this particular criticism — with narrower slots, a length of folded wire could be sewed into the other end of the strap which could then be threaded through and held firmly, but easily removable.

If the arm brace was thought to have commercial potential, this would be considered a major advantage because the actual arm brace and straps could be manufactured independant of one another. Perhaps the most commercially appealing aspect of this design is its simplicity and improved production techniques, synonymous with large scale manufacture, would have no difficulty in producing the artefact efficiently in terms of materials, labour and time.

Unfortunately however, the simplicity factor is reliant on the fact that it was designed specifically to satisfy my grandfather's unique requirements, a similar arm brace for wider distribution would necessitate the inclusion of some method of adjustment — adding further, unwanted complexity. I also doubt the existence of a suitable market to justify such manufacture, nevertheless, perhaps there is sufficient demand to warrant limited production on an individual scale.

The completed arm brace must be assessed in its capacity as a prototype which is, as such, subject to simplifications and modifications:

A greater degree of development of the brachioradialis muscle is common, i.e. lower arm diameter has a much greater range than that of the upper arm. This was known, but not considered, beforehand.

- Biceps
- Brachialis
- Brachioradialis

| | Evaluation | Sheet No. 46 | | |

Acknowledgements:

Mr. I.E. Jones : for his readiness to co-operate at every opportunity.

Mr. H. Stanley
Mr. W.B. Maple } for guidance and advice in their capacity as consultants.

Mrs. H. Stanley : machine sewing.

Mr. M. Pritchard-Howarth : photography.

Camp Ltd., Portfield Ind. Estate, Nevil Shute Rd, Portsmouth, Hants.

Disabled living foundation's information service, 380/384 Harrow Rd, London W9

Hugh Steeper (Roehampton) Ltd, 59 North Worple Way, Mortlake, London SW14 8PS.

Visiting Aids Centre, 16 Fitzroy Square, London WIP 5HQ

Institute for consumer ergonomics, University of Technology, Loughborough, Leics, LE11 CJB

The DHSS Store, Health Publications Unit, Heywood, Lancs, OL10 2PZ

The Arthritis and Rheumatism Council, 41 Eagle Street, London WC1R 4AR.

Mecanaids Ltd, Gloucester, GL1 1BR

Homecraft Supplies, 27 Trinity Road, London SW17 7SF.

Bibliography:

Out on a limb, a celebration of the British Limbless Ex-Service Men's Association Golden Jubilee 1932-1982

Housing interiors for the disabled and elderly, by Bettyann Boetticher Raschko.

| | Acknowledgements and Bibliography | Sheet No. 47 | | |

1.3 Examiner's comments

GENERAL COMMENTS

a) A well-organised Folio with a list of contents and each sheet is numbered.
b) Writing is easy to read and the drawings are clear, well detailed and easy to understand.
c) Each section, i.e. Situation, Specification, Investigation, Solutions, Realisation, Evaluation, etc., are all clearly labelled.
d) The depth and detail of each section is very thorough.
e) Good use has been made of personal sketching, photographs, Three- and two-dimensional drawings, Orthographic Projection and section views.
f) Evaluation well detailed with recommendations for improvements.

SPECIFIC COMMENTS

a) A valid and worthwhile need had been identified.
b) Constraints of cost and time recognised.
c) Research/investigation very thorough and appropriate.
d) Variety of solutions pursued.
e) Technical and constructional knowledge very sound.
f) Annotations give reasons for selection and rejection of ideas.
g) British Standards PP 7308 recommendations well understood and appropriately applied.
h) Evaluative judgements of each solution perceptive and thorough.
i) Final evaluation very thorough.
j) Acknowledgements help to demonstrate the thoroughness this project has received.
k) The inclusion of a Bibliography helps to emphasise the care and thorough attention this project received.

UNIT 2 SHADOW THEATRE

2.1 Problem set by LEAG (assessment weighting 15%)

Each year a topic or theme is given during the final year of the course. The candidate has time to collect information and to present it as part of the coursework in an *Investigation and Research Folio*. The candidate then selects one problem from three set by the Examining Group. This is completed on Design Answer Sheets provided by the Examining Group.

Theme: Movement in two planes

Problem: Shadow Theatre

Shadow theatres were popular toys in the past. The shadow of the characters were thrown on to a translucent screen or proscenium. The characters or puppets were animated by systems of levers and linkages so that quite complex movements and effects could be achieved.

Your shadow theatre should

a) have a proscenium not larger than an A3 sheet of paper;
b) have two animated characters which can be operated without obscuring the screen;
c) have characters selected from a suitable story, nursery rhyme, or fairy story suitable for young children; the story must be specified in your brief;
d) be robust and withstand use by young children.

2.2 Student's answer

1. *(a)* State the problem chosen.

Shadow Theatre: Little Miss Muffet

(b) Summary of your Folio (Research and Investigation).

1) Visited local school & play group
2) Found out favourite nursery rhyme
3) Read books on Shadow Theatres
4) Visited Bethnalgreen Museum
5) Asked older people about shadow theatres
6) Types of lighting
7) Materials for the screen
8) How to make silhouettes
9) Levers and linkages

(c) Analysis of the Problem.

List the important points that you will consider in preparing your design.

The design must be
a) Suitable for children between the ages of 3 & 5 years
b) Suitable for approximately 10 children to watch
c) Suitable for two children to operate
d) placed on a table
e) folded flat when stored away
f) attractive.

Specifications
a) Proscenium must not be larger than A3 paper
b) Have two animated characters which can be operated without obscuring the screen
c) Have characters illustrating Little Miss Muffet
d) Be robust.

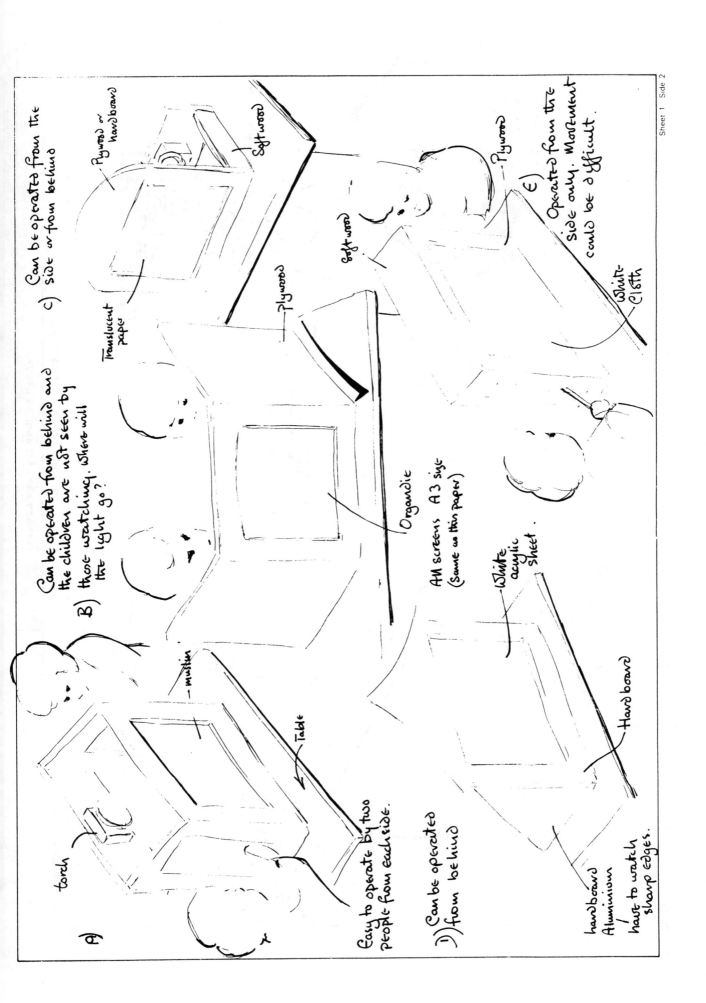

a)

torch

Easy to operate by two people from each side.

1) Can be operated from behind

hardboard
Aluminium
have to watch
sharp edges.

B) Can be operated from behind and the children are not seen by those watching. Where will the light go?

c) Can be operated from the side or from behind

Plywood or hardboard

Soft wood

Translucent paper

Plywood

Soft wood

muslin

Table

Organdie

All screens A3 size (same as thin paper)

White acrylic Sheet.

Hardboard

E) Operated from the side only. Movement could be difficult.

Plywood

White C18th

1151/1

MY FIRST IDEAS AND DECISIONS ARE:

(Put a tick against those ideas you are going to use)

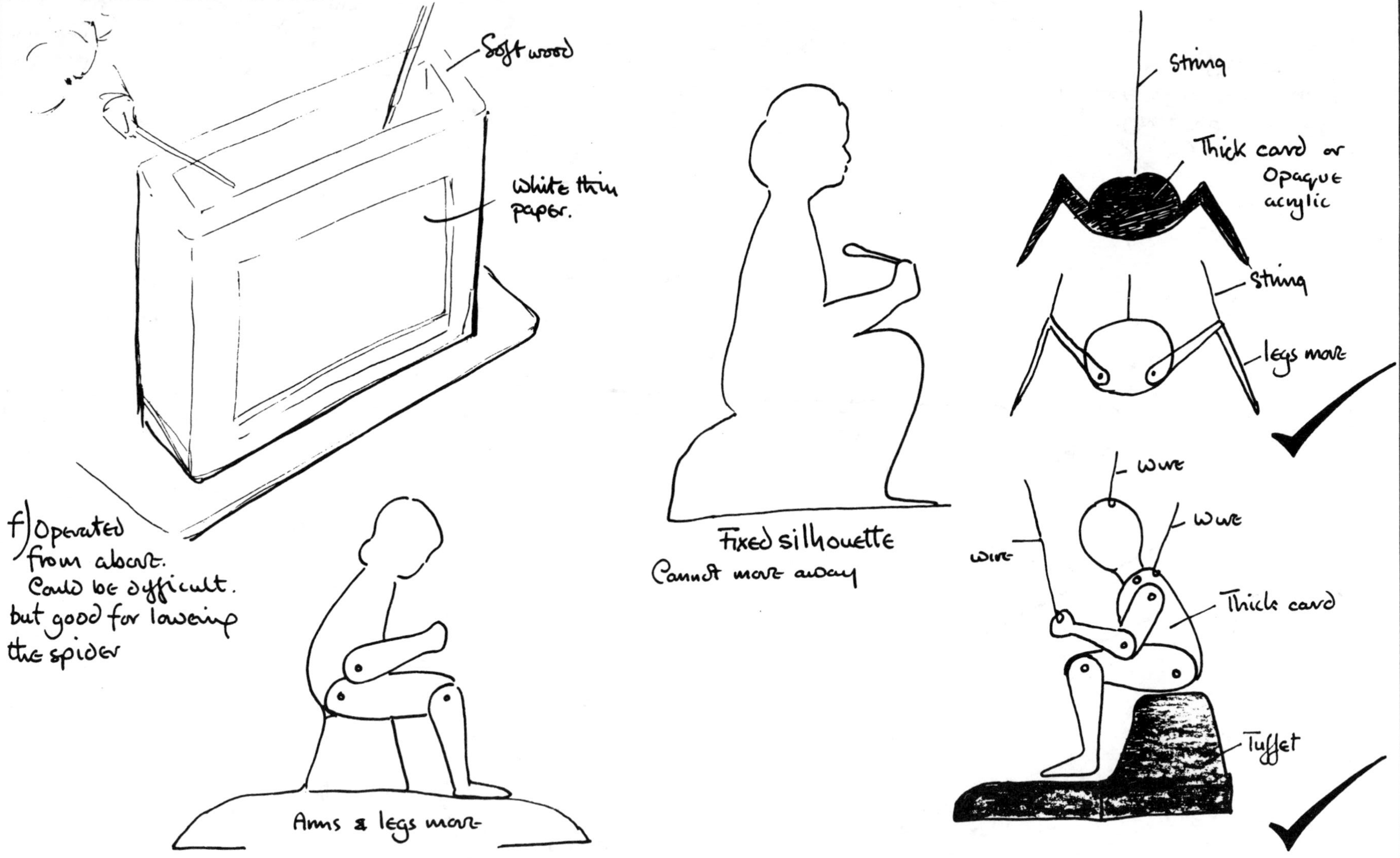

Soft wood

White thin paper.

f) Operated from above. Could be difficult. but good for lowering the spider

String

Thick card or Opaque acrylic

String

legs move

wire

wire

Thick card

wire

Tuffet

wire

Fixed silhouette

Cannot move away

Arms & legs move-

---

2. INITIAL IDEAS		ADD DETAIL OF THE MATERIALS TO BE USED.
Paper 1: Design and Realisation	GCSE CDT: DESIGN AND REALISATION	CENTRE No. .... CANDIDATE No. ....
You can use the back of this sheet if you require more space	LONDON AND EAST ANGLIAN GROUP	CANDIDATE NAME ....

Sheet 2   Side 1   [*Turn over*

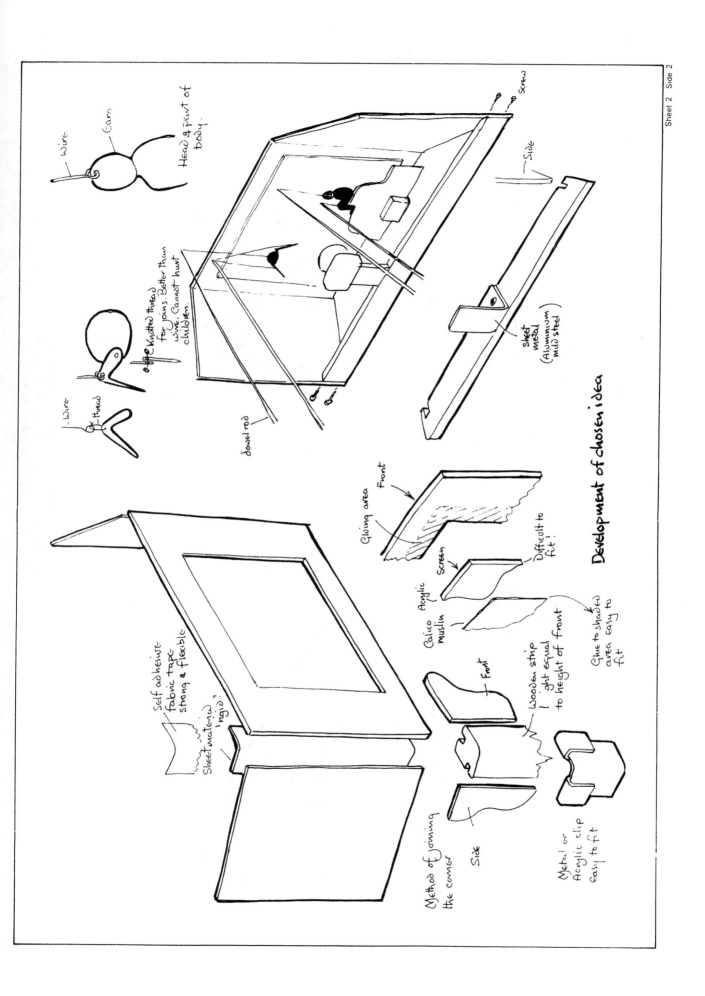

Wire

Ears

Head & part of body.

Wire

Thread

Head

Knotted thread for joins. Better than wire. Cannot hurt children.

Dowel rod

Screw

Side

Sheet metal (Aluminium/mild steel)

Front

Gluing area

Calico Acrylic Muslin

Screen

Difficult to fit!

Glue to shaded area easy to fit

Front

Wooden strip height equal to height of front

Self adhesive fabric tape strong & flexible

Sheet material 'rigid'?

Side

Method of joining the corner

Metal or Acrylic clip easy to fit

Development of chosen idea

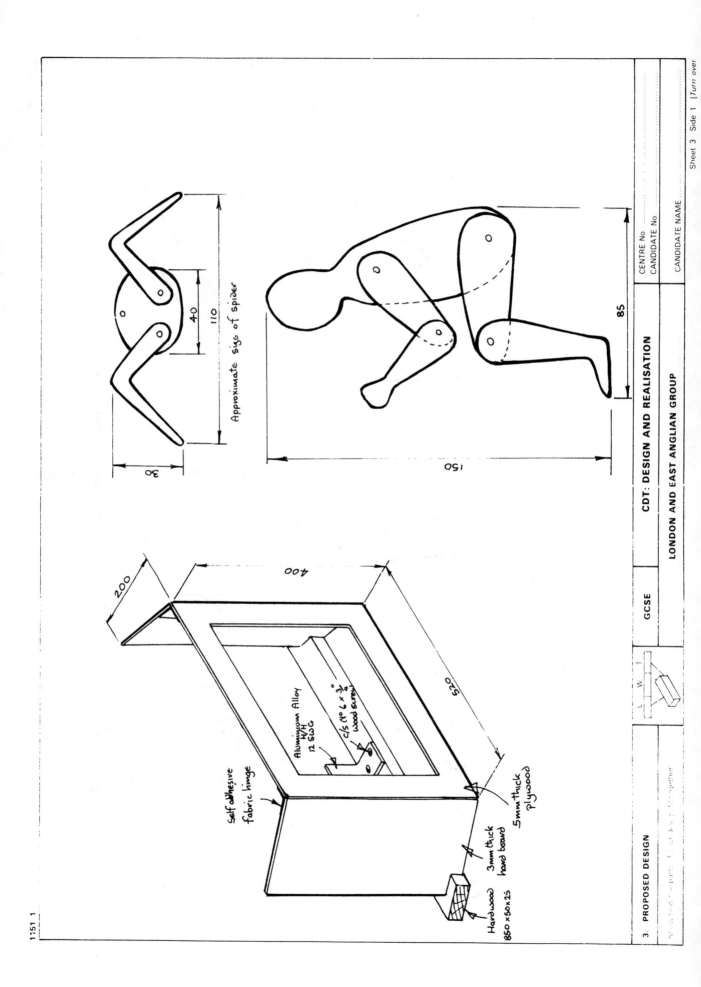

3. PROPOSED DESIGN

GCSE

CDT: DESIGN AND REALISATION

LONDON AND EAST ANGLIAN GROUP

CENTRE No
CANDIDATE No
CANDIDATE NAME

Sheet 3 Side 1 *Turn over*

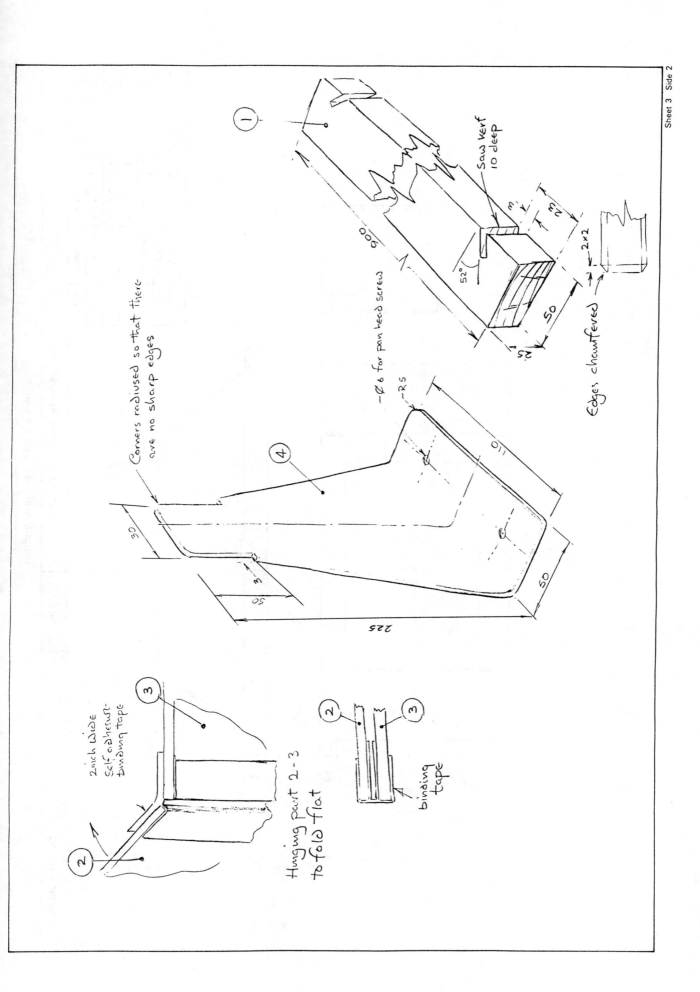

ORIGINAL SCALE 1 : 5

PROJECTION

PART Nº	NAME	MATERIAL	SIZE	Nº OFF
6	Screen	Organdie	450×335	1
5	Cycle torch			1
4	Torch bracket	Aluminium	275 × 110 × 16 SWG	1
3	Front	Plywood	825 × 400 × 5	1
2	Side	Hardboard	400 × 250 × 3	2
1	Back support	Beech	900 × 50 × 25	1

CENTRE No.	....
CANDIDATE No.	....

CANDIDATE NAME ....

4. WORKING DRAWING	GCSE	**CDT: DESIGN AND REALISATION**

LONDON AND EAST ANGLIAN GROUP

Use this sheet for your working drawing and material requirements

1151/1

Sheet 4

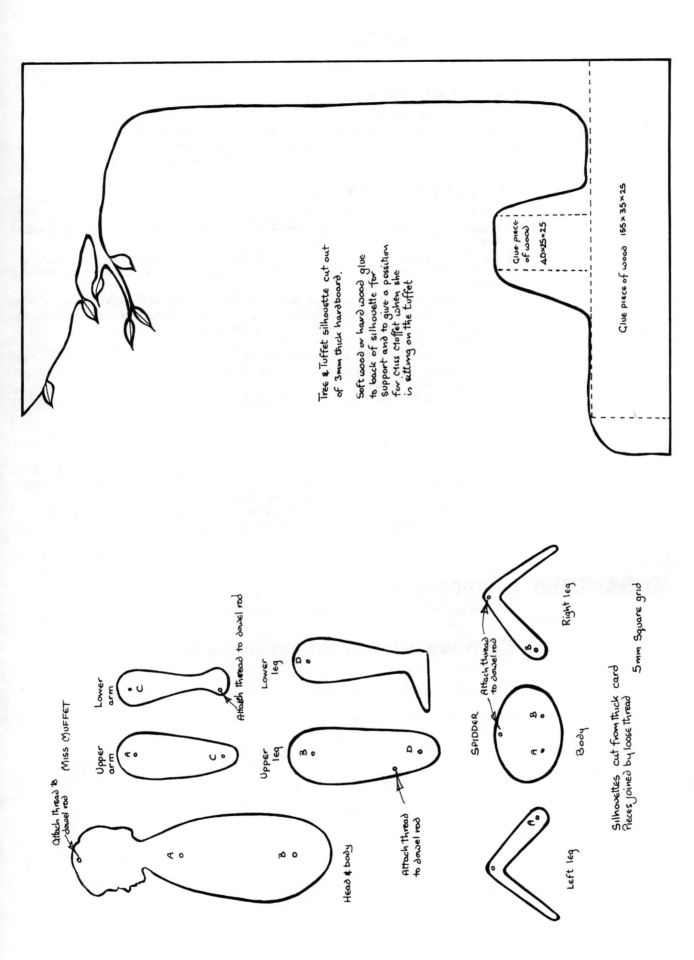

Tree & Tuffet silhouette cut out of 3mm thick hardboard.

Soft wood or hard wood glue to back of silhouette for support and to give a position for Miss Moffet when she is sitting on the tuffet

Glue piece of wood 40×25×25

Glue piece of wood 155×35×25

MISS MUFFET

Upper arm

Lower arm

A

C

C

Attach thread to dowel rod

Attach thread to dowel rod

Lower leg

D

Upper leg

B

D

Attach thread to dowel rod

Head & body

A

B

Attach thread to dowel rod

SPIDDER

Attach thread to dowel rod

Body

A

B

Right leg

B

Left leg

A

Silhouettes cut from thick card
Pieces joined by loose thread

5mm Square grid

2.3 Examiner's comments

GENERAL COMMENTS

a) All aspects completed.
b) Neatly and clearly presented without excessive use of writing.
c) Gives the impression that a feasible solution has been achieved.
d) Good use has been made of two and three dimensional drawings.

SPECIFIC COMMENTS

a) Problem stated and a nursery rhyme given.
b) Summary of research clearly presented showing that the relevant areas of research and investigation had been covered.
c) The list includes all the points that could be reasonably expected in an analysis.
d) A good variety of ideas for the theatre but a limited range of ideas for the animated characters.
e) Annotations helpful by naming material and some design observation such as 'easy to fit', 'can be operated from behind by two children', 'fixed silhouette cannot move away', etc., showing that the candidate is thinking.
f) Constructional detail well presented in exploded three-dimensional views.
g) Development of chosen idea thoroughly thought out and constructional detail basic but adequate and appropriate for the problem. Dimensions and name of materials appropriate and feasible.
h) Good use made of Orthographic Projection for the theatre and square grid paper for the animated characters.

CONCLUSION

This candidate has presented sufficient evidence to show that he or she is able to carry out appropriate investigation, present information in an orderly fashion, communicate ideas, knowledge, design reasoning, briefly and clearly.

This is a level of work that is well above average and could expect to get an A grade if all the other aspects of the course are of the same standard.

> **UNIT 3** MOTOR-POWERED TOY

3.1 Problem set by LEAG (assessment weighting 15%)

Theme: Simple energy conversions

Problem: Motor-powered toy

3.2 Student's answer

1. (a) State the problem chosen.
DESIGN A TOY FOR THE AGE GROUP, 3-6 YEARS POWERED BY
A SAFE BATTERY+MOTOR SOURCE.THE TOY SHOULD HAVE
MOVING PARTS AND IS TO BE SELF-CONTAINED IN THAT
BATTERY,SWITCH AND MOTOR ARE ON OR WITHIN THE TOY
ITSELF.

(b) Summary of your investigation. (Folio)

SOURCES OF ENERGY
SUN,WIND,WATER,FOSSIL FUELS(OIL,COAL,NATURAL GAS).
TYPES OF ENERGY
HEAT,LIGHT,SOUND,ELECTRICAL,CHEMICAL,MECHANICAL.
STORAGE OF KINETIC ENERGY
POTENTIAL ENERGY,EXAMPLES OF STORING ENERGY,ENERGY
EQUATIONS.
CONVERSION OF ENERGY
HEAT-LIGHT,MECHANICAL-ELECTRICAL.
ENERGY-MOTION
ROTARY,LINEAR RECIPROCATING.
CONTROL OF ENERGY
SWITCHES,RESISTORS,DIODES,VARIABLE RESISTORS,MECHANISMS.

(c) Analysis of the Problem.

List the important points that you will consider in preparing your design

1.HOW CAN THE MOTORS SPEED BE INCREASED/REDUCED?

2.HOW WILL AXLES TURN FREELY AND FRICTION BE REDUCED?

3.HOW CAN THE TOY BE TURNED OFF AND ON?

4.WHAT MATERIALS SHOULD BE USED IN MAKING THE TOY?

5.SHOULD THE BATTERY BE ACCESSABLE?

6.HOW CAN THE ROTARY MOTION OF THE MOTOR BE CONVERTED IN
LINEAR AND RECIPROCATING MOTION?

SPUR GEARS

48 Teeth   16 Teeth

Speed Change ;3 Times Faster

For Same Direction Rotation

$$\frac{\text{Number Of Teeth On Motor Gear}}{\text{Number Of Teeth On Driven Gear}} = \frac{\text{Speed Of Driven Gear}}{\text{Speed Of Motor Gear}}$$

$$\text{Gear ratio} = \frac{\text{number of teeth on driven gear}}{\text{number of teeth on motor gear}}$$

90° MOTION CHANGE

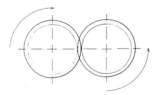

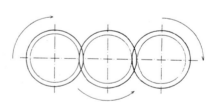

BEVEL GEARS

WORM+SPUR GEAR

FLEXIBLE BELT PULLEY

RECIPROCATING MOTION

PULLEYS

For Opposite Direction Rotation

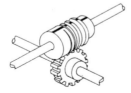

$$\frac{\text{DIAMETER OF MOTOR PULLEY}}{\text{DIAMETER OF DRIVEN PULLEY}} = \frac{\text{SPEED OF DRIVEN PULLEY}}{\text{SPEED OF MOTOR PULLEY}}$$

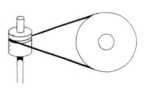

CAM

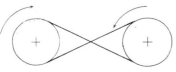

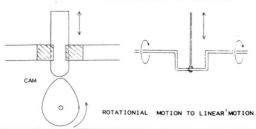

ROTATIONAL MOTION TO LINEAR MOTION

MY FIRST IDEAS AND DECISIONS ARE
(Put a tick against those ideas you are going to use.)

FRONT WHEEL AXLE : 90° MOTION CHANGE

FRONT WHEEL AXLE : UP/DOWN MOTION

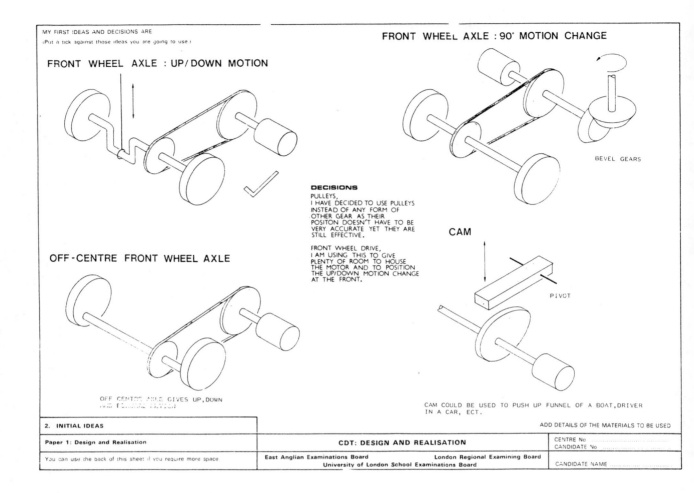

BEVEL GEARS

DECISIONS

PULLEYS,
I HAVE DECIDED TO USE PULLEYS
INSTEAD OF ANY FORM OF
OTHER GEAR AS THEIR
POSITON DOESN'T HAVE TO BE
VERY ACCURATE YET THEY ARE
STILL EFFECTIVE.

FRONT WHEEL DRIVE,
I AM USING THIS TO GIVE
PLENTY OF ROOM TO HOUSE
THE MOTOR AND TO POSITION
THE UP/DOWN MOTION CHANGE
AT THE FRONT.

OFF-CENTRE FRONT WHEEL AXLE

CAM

PIVOT

OFF CENTRE AXLE GIVES UP, DOWN
AND FORWARD MOTION

CAM COULD BE USED TO PUSH UP FUNNEL OF A BOAT, DRIVER
IN A CAR, ECT.

2. INITIAL IDEAS		ADD DETAILS OF THE MATERIALS TO BE USED
Paper 1: Design and Realisation	**CDT: DESIGN AND REALISATION**	CENTRE No .... CANDIDATE No ....
You can use the back of this sheet if you require more space	East Anglian Examinations Board London Regional Examining Board University of London School Examinations Board	CANDIDATE NAME ....

TRAIN

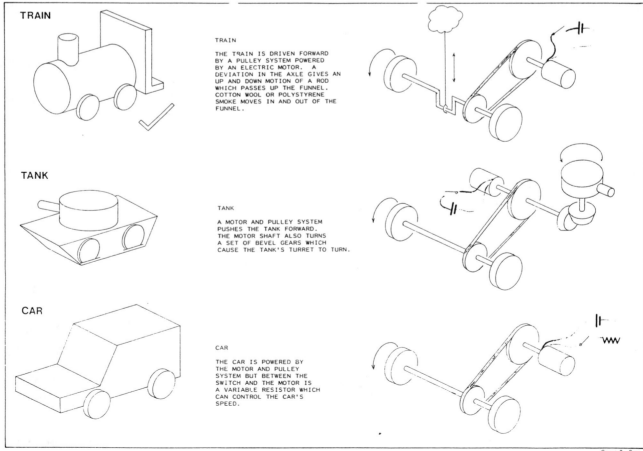

TRAIN

THE TRAIN IS DRIVEN FORWARD
BY A PULLEY SYSTEM POWERED
BY AN ELECTRIC MOTOR. A
DEVIATION IN THE AXLE GIVES AN
UP AND DOWN MOTION OF A ROD
WHICH PASSES UP THE FUNNEL.
COTTON WOOL OR POLYSTYRENE
SMOKE MOVES IN AND OUT OF THE
FUNNEL.

TANK

TANK

A MOTOR AND PULLEY SYSTEM
PUSHES THE TANK FORWARD.
THE MOTOR SHAFT ALSO TURNS
A SET OF BEVEL GEARS WHICH
CAUSE THE TANK'S TURRET TO TURN.

CAR

CAR

THE CAR IS POWERED BY
THE MOTOR AND PULLEY
SYSTEM BUT BETWEEN THE
SWITCH AND THE MOTOR IS
A VARIABLE RESISTOR WHICH
CAN CONTROL THE CAR'S
SPEED.

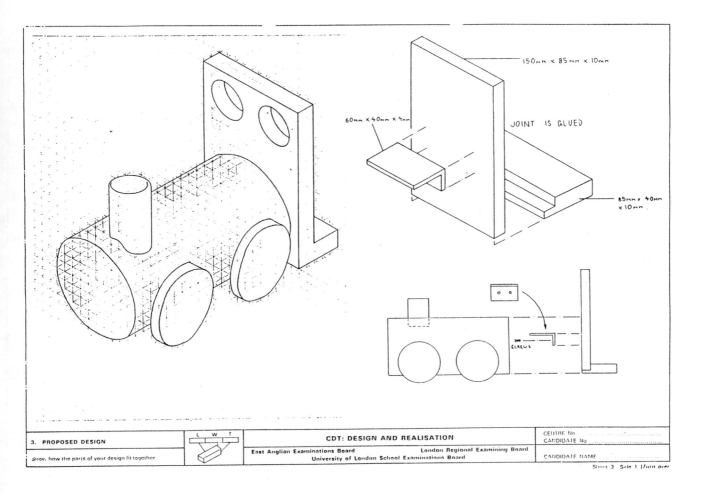

3. PROPOSED DESIGN	L W T	CDT: DESIGN AND REALISATION	CENTRE No CANDIDATE No
Show how the parts of your design fit together		East Anglian Examinations Board London Regional Examining Board University of London School Examinations Board	CANDIDATE NAME

Sheet 3 Side 1 *Turn over*

150mm x 85mm x 10mm

60mm x 40mm x 4mm

JOINT IS GLUED

85mm x 40mm x 10mm.

SCREWS

FUNNEL.
THE FUNNEL HAS A NARROW
INNER GAP SO THAT THE PUSH
ROD TRAVELS MORE
DIRECTLY UP AND DOWN
RATHER THAN ROTATIONALLY.

Ø30mm x 45mm

MOTOR

SWITCH

BATTERY (1.5V)

HOLE FOR WIRES

Ø70mm x
10mm

Ø85mm x 170mm

GLUED

Ø85mm x
5mm

MOTOR

Ø20

Ø90

Sheet 3 Side 2

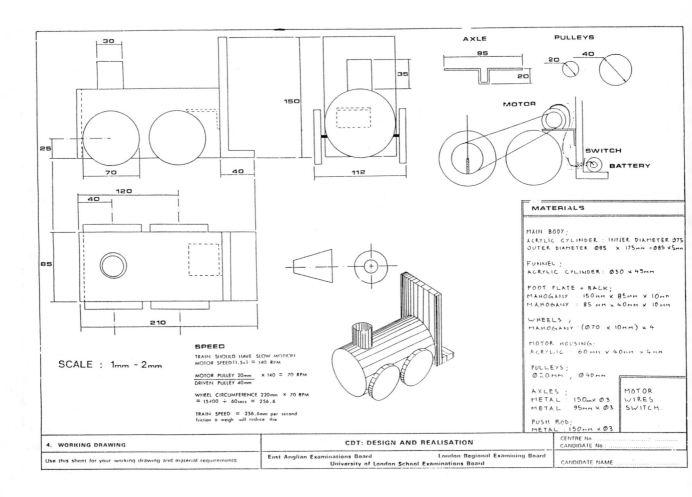

GENERAL COMMENTS

a) An exceptionally high quality level of presentation.
b) All aspects attempted.
c) Investigation mainly into mechanisms.
d) Good use made of Isometric Projection.

SPECIFIC COMMENTS

a) A fully stated Design Brief.
b) Summary of investigation has concentrated on the mechanical, electrical and electronic aspects only. The needs and interest of the child have not been mentioned.
c) The analysis of the problem again concentrates on the mechanical function and nothing that relates to the child.
d) Development of the ideas is narrow, i.e. the train, tank and car are just variations of transport all of which depend on a four wheel system.
e) The variation of gears, and the use of a cam to change direction of movement, shows that this aspect has been deeply considered.
f) While the gearing detail is quite thorough the constructional detail of the toy is far from complete.
g) The working drawing shows a good understanding of Orthographic Projection though some conventional detail is missing, e.g. the arrow heads on the end of dimensions, and the method of presenting the scale should be given as a ratio and not include units of measurement.
h) Use could have been made of numbering the parts so that they relate to the details given in the cutting list.

3.3 Examiner's comments

CONCLUSION

This candidate is able to present information graphically to a very high level and would be well rewarded for communication skills. However, because such aspects as the needs of the child appeared to have been forgotten, some constructional detail missing, and the very limited range of ideas presented for the toys, the designing aspects are not at such a high level as the graphics. This means that what appeared to be a top level piece of work at first is lacking in other areas and will be assessed slightly lower. This level of work is still well above average and could expect to just get a B grade providing the other aspects of the course reflected at least a similar standard.

UNIT 4 CONTAINER OR SYSTEM FOR STORING ITEMS

4.1 Problem set by WJEC

Everything in its place

Storage is often a problem. Sometimes the difficulty can be overcome by following the old saying a place for everything and everything in its place. This applies to almost everything from large bulky objects down to things as tiny as a pin.

Think of a particular situation where you know storage is a problem, for example in your home, in the shed or garage, at school, at a club you belong to.

Investigate the problem. Identify the items that need storing.

Using any suitable combination of materials, design a container (or some system) that can be used to store those items safely and tidily.

In your design solution there must be a place for everything. It must be easy to remove and replace each individual item.

4.2 Student's answer

CONTENTS   Page N°

DESIGN BRIEF AND ANALYSIS   2

RESEARCH AND INVESTIGATION   3, 4 & 5

DEVELOPMENT OF IDEAS   6

DEVELOPMENT OF CHOSEN IDEA   7

WORKING DRAWING   8

CUTTING LIST   8

EVALUATION   9

SHEET N°   I

DESIGN BRIEF

Design a container or system for storing items

Analysis

a) The items must be stored safely.

b) The items must be :—

(i) easy to identify;
(ii) easy to remove;
(iii) easy to replace;
(iv) kept tidy.

c) Can be made from more than one material.

d) Must be able to be made by me in the school workshops.

e) Must be able to be completed by........

SHEET No 2

STORAGE AT HOME

Wardrobe for clothes

Chest of drawers.

Kitchen drawers & cupboards

Cups hanging on hooks in the kitchen

Knives
Forks
Spoons
Small spoons
Small forks
Drawer removed

metal hooks

Garden spade & Garden fork hanging on the wall of the shed.

Dad's tool box

NEED

Video tapes
Video

NEED

Coffee table covered with magazines

RESEARCH & INVESTIGATION TO IDENTIFY A NEED   SHEET No 3

ITEMS TO BE STORED :   10 Videocassette tapes.

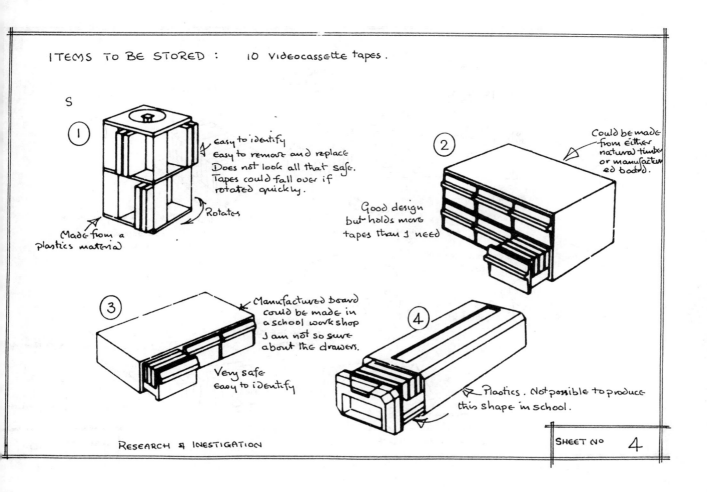

S

① Easy to identify
Easy to remove and replace
Does not look all that safe.
Tapes could fall over if rotated quickly.

Rotates

Made from a plastics material

② Could be made from either natural timber or manufactured board.

Good design but holds more tapes than I need

③ Manufactured board could be made in a school workshop I am not so sure about the drawers.

Very safe
Easy to identify

④ Plastics. Not possible to produce this shape in school.

RESEARCH & INVESTIGATION

SHEET NO   4

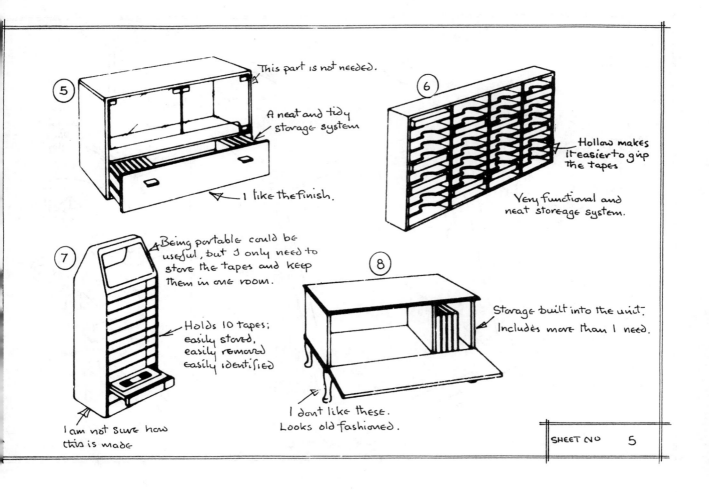

⑤ This part is not needed.

A neat and tidy storage system

I like the finish.

⑥ Hollow makes it easier to grip the tapes

Very functional and neat storeage system.

⑦ Being portable could be useful, but I only need to store the tapes and keep them in one room.

Holds 10 tapes; easily stored, easily removed easily identified

I am not sure how this is made

⑧ Storage built into the unit. Includes more than I need.

I don't like these. Looks old fashioned.

SHEET NO   5

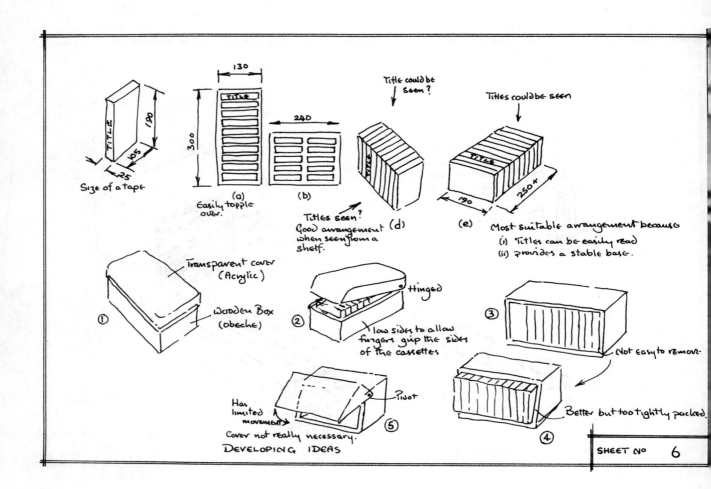

Size of a tape

130

300

240

(a) Easily topple over.

(b)

(d) Titles seen? Good arrangement when seen from a shelf.

Title could be seen?

(e) Titles could be seen

190   250+

Most suitable arrangement because
(i) Titles can be easily read
(ii) provides a stable base.

① Transparent cover (Acrylic)
Wooden Box (obeche)

② Hinged
low sides to allow fingers grip the sides of the cassettes

③

④ Not easy to remove
Better but too tightly packed.

⑤ Has limited movement
Pivot
Cover not really necessary.

DEVELOPING IDEAS

SHEET NO   6

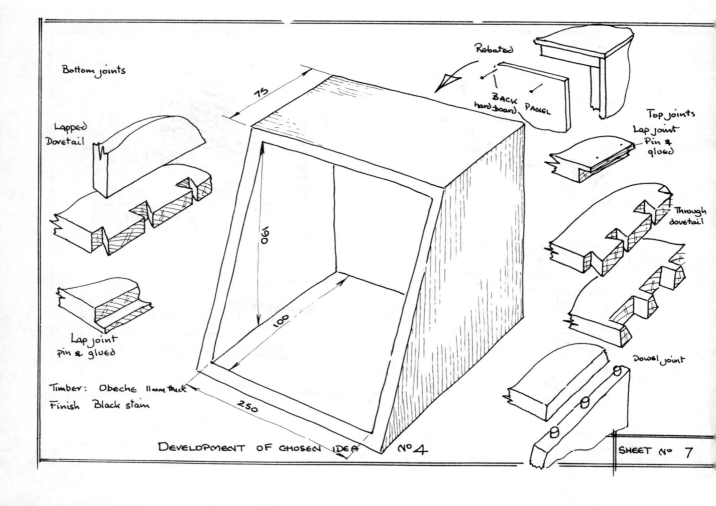

Bottom joints

Lapped Dovetail

Lap joint pin & glued

75

190

100

250

Timber: Obeche 11mm thick
Finish   Black stain

Rebated

BACK hard board   PANEL

Top joints
Lap joint
Pin & glued

Through dovetail

Dowel joint

DEVELOPMENT OF CHOSEN IDEA   N°4

SHEET NO   7

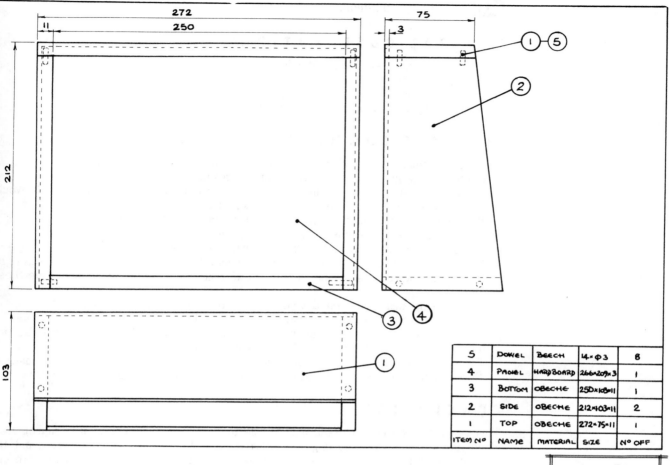

5	DOWEL	BEECH	14×⌀3	8
4	PANEL	HARDBOARD	266×209×3	1
3	BOTTOM	OBECHE	250×108×11	1
2	SIDE	OBECHE	212×103×11	2
1	TOP	OBECHE	272×75×11	1
ITEM Nº	NAME	MATERIAL	SIZE	Nº OFF

SHEET Nº 8

Design Brief :   Design a container or system for storing ten videocassette tapes

Criteria of Assessment   Comment

a) Can the cassetts be stored safely ?   Yes. Because they are protected by the contain. made from a hard wood.

b) (i) Can the tapes be easily identified ?   Yes. Because the title edge is facing outwards.

   (ii) Can the tapes be easily removed ?   No. They are too tightly packed together. (see recommendation)

   (iii) Can the tapes be easily put back ?   No. The last tape to put back is always difficult. Too tightly packed.

   (iv) Are the tapes easy to keep tidy ?   Yes. They stay in place when stored.

c) Was the material suitable ?   Yes. The wood is strong and was easy to work.

d) Was it easy to make ?   Yes. The most difficult part was planing the end grain but
                                             the joint went cleanly together when cramped.

e) Was it able to be made in the time available ?   Yes. I finished it and was able to concentrate on giving it a
                                             good finish

f) If I was going to, have to make this container again I would make the following recommendations :-

Recommendation   Reason

1. Make the container slightly larger   So that I could get a better grip of the tape and it would slide in
                                             or out without disturbing the other tapes.

2. Put a dividing piece of hardboard   This would keep the tapes slightly appart. They would then be easier
   between each tape.   to put in and out.   SHEET Nº   9

4.3 Examiner's comments

GENERAL OBSERVATIONS

a) An orderly and well organised folio.
b) All aspects attempted.
c) Easy to follow.
d) Content appears to be a little thin for a 12-month project.

SPECIFIC COMMENTS

a) Cover contains the most important detail with the minimum of fuss.
b) Contents clearly listed and page numbers given.
c) Design Brief written as a summary of the problem and not really a brief. It would appear that a need has not yet been identified.
d) Research and investigation for a need quite broad but not deep.
e) A need has been identified, i.e. 'To store ten videocassette tapes'.
f) Research goes little beyond looking at existing designs.
g) Has approached the problem in a practical way by examining the different ways the tapes can be arranged and notes show that good and bad points have been identified.
h) The chosen idea has been developed to show how it can be made.
i) A few alternative methods of construction have been considered.
j) Working drawing adequately detailed. Sound understanding of Orthographic Projection and correct use of British Standards recommendations.
k) Evaluative judgements are made referring back to the Design Brief and analysis. Recommendations are made where necessary and accompanied by reasons.

CONCLUSION

This candidate is well organised and is able to complete the process of designing from identifying a need to evaluating the solution. All stages have been covered and the contents show a basic understanding of designing and a knowledge of working with one material. The amount and depth of study is limited. Having worked in a single material may be sufficient to stop this candidate getting a C grade. To be sure of a C and higher grade you should show that you can think and make solutions that use a range of materials.

UNIT 5 | EXAMPLES OF REALISATION

When the examiner is assessing the product or artefact that you have made, he or she is looking for four main areas:

▶ Finish
▶ Accuracy
▶ Complexity
▶ Techniques.

You can remember these areas by the initials: FACT. There is no particular order in which these will be assessed but an examiner will form an overall impression and then look carefully at each of the areas mentioned. You don't have the advantage of seeing the end products and only have the following photographs from which to form judgements.

Remember the assessor is only assessing the making skills and not the designing skills when assessing the quality of the end product.

5.1 Cycle kit storage unit (Fig 4.2)

▶ **Finish:** all surfaces have been sealed and neatly painted.
▶ **Accuracy:** all parts are joined together securely, equipment is held in place by well-fitted compartments, and the doors open and close without any problem.

▶ **Complexity**: the quantity of work and degree of difficulty is sufficiently demanding for an able student. Joining corners at 45° is more difficult that joining materials at 90°.

▶ **Techniques**: appropriate construction techniques have been used to make this project. (This detail cannot be seen clearly from the photograph but when a project has been made using the appropriate techniques it will usually function well and be strong enough to do the job it is intended to do.)

This level of work is what is expected from an A/B grade candidate.

5.2 Stationery storage unit (Fig 4.3)

▶ **Finish**: completed and quite well done.
▶ **Accuracy**: all parts fit and function well, i.e. doors fit and drawers move easily and smoothly.
▶ **Complexity**: a very demanding piece of work.
▶ **Techniques**: appropriate methods applied and successfully completed.

Level A/B.

5.3 Bottle storage unit (Fig 4.4)

▶ **Finish**: excellent.
▶ **Accuracy**: very high standard.
▶ **Complexity**: very demanding for even the most able candidate.
▶ **Technique**: the method employed was the same as that used by a cooper, i.e. slats of wood are held together to form a cylinder. A specialised technique expertly carried out.

Level A.

5.4 Novelty litter bin (Fig 4.5)

▶ **Mock-ups and models**: here is an example of practical work that could be assessed by the work done to produce the models. The design of the final product was more appropriate to industrial methods of production and therefore it was not feasible for the candidate to produce a full-size bin. The scale model, however, shows that this was an able candidate.

Level A/B.

5.5 Children's novelty storage unit (Fig 4.6)

▶ **Finish**: this is a large project that had been well finished on all surfaces.
▶ **Accuracy**: a completed project in which all moving parts fit and all joining surfaces fit accurately.
▶ **Complexity**: there is a lot of repetitive work, i.e. five drawers, which is more demanding on the candidate's ability to remain constantly accurate than upon his or her ability to perform a range of quite varied skills. On balance this is a very demanding piece of work.
▶ **Techniques**: the construction and materials are robust and well able to withstand being used by children.

5.6 Inspiration from insects (Fig 4.7)

▶ **Finish**: the casting resins and the moulded plastics used required a high level of finish in the moulds, so that little had to be done to the actual end product. The base was carefully prepared and painted.

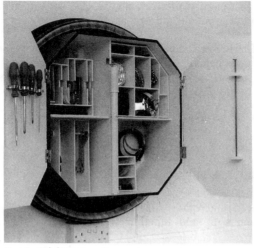

Fig 4.2   Cycle kit storage unit

Fig 4.3   Stationery storage unit

Fig 4.4   Bottle storage unit

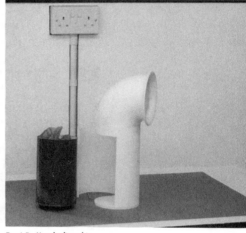

Fig 4.5   Novelty litter bin

Fig 4.6   Children's novelty storage unit

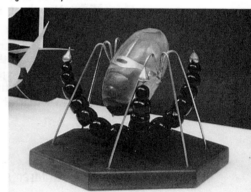

Fig 4.7   Inspiration from insects

Fig 4.8   Educational game for four people

Fig 4.9   Walking aid

▶ **Accuracy**: the fact that all parts go together and achieve the desired form is a good indication of accurate measurement.
▶ **Complexity**: the most difficult part of producing an end product of this form is in the making of the moulds, and to be able to produce a form of this kind is quite complex and demanding.
▶ **Technique**: quite a wide range of making skills needed to work in wood, metal and plastics.

Level A/B.

5.7 Educational game for four people (Fig 4.8)

▶ **Finish**: all wooden surfaces have been sealed with a varnish and the end product's appearance is much improved.
▶ **Accuracy**: the fitting together of so many small components required a high degree of accuracy.
▶ **Complexity**: quite demanding for an able candidate.
▶ **Techniques**: appropriate and well suited to the design.

Level A.

5.8 Walking aid (Fig 4.9)

▶ **Finish**: the main frame is adequately painted, but a tube end is not capped and the front leg requires a finish to stop corrosion.
▶ **Accuracy**: the electromagnetic switch functioned efficiently and the leg adjustment moved smoothly within the main frame. The joins were sound, clearly indicating that accuracy was of a high level.
▶ **Complexity**: this is a sufficiently demanding project for an able pupil.
▶ **Techniques**: tube bending and welding most appropriate for the main frame. Lathe work and bench work appropriately applied for the production of the electromagnetic adjustment device.

Level A/B.

UNIT 6   CONCLUSION

You must remember that grades are not awarded for individual pieces of work and that a grade is only awarded when every part of the course has been assessed and marked. The grades awarded for the example Design Folios and the example realisations are only given to show you the level of work that would be expected for that grade.

Remember that it is *you* that is being assessed, and the work that you produce is the evidence of your ability. What the work does not show to a stranger, such as a visiting assessor, is how much of the evidence results from your efforts and how much from your teacher's. Such aspects as planning, safety, and an ability to work as a result of your own initiative, are not always evident in the final work. So your teacher, who *has* seen you work, is able to make these judgements and to take these factors into account when assessing your work.